Brutal

This book is dedicated to the boys from the Brook.
Those who survived,
Those who didn't
And those who were never found.

The Crow.

Brutal

Surviving Westbrook Boys Home

Al 'Crow' Fletcher's story
as told to Cheryl Jorgensen

Who guards the guards?
(from Juvenal's Satires circa 115 AD)

NEW
HOLLAND

www.newholland.com.au

Published in Australia in 2006 by
New Holland Publishers (Australia) Pty Ltd
Sydney • Auckland • London • Cape Town
www.newholland.com.au

14 Aquatic Drive Frenchs Forest NSW 2086 Australia
218 Lake Road Northcote Auckland New Zealand
86 Edgware Road London W2 2EA United Kingdom
80 McKenzie Street Cape Town 8001 South Africa
Copyright © in text: Al Fletcher and Cheryl Jorgensen, 2004
Copyright © 2005 New Holland Publishers (Australia) Pty Ltd

National Library of Australia Cataloguing-in-Publication Data:
Fletcher, Alfred.

  Brutal.

  Revised.
  ISBN 1 74110 416 5.

  1. Fletcher, Alfred. 2. Westbrook Training Centre
  (Toowoomba, Qld.). 3. Juvenile delinquents - Queensland -
  Biography. 4. Adult child abuse victims - Queensland -
  Biography. 5. Prisoners' writings, Australian. I.
  Jorgensen, Cheryl. II. Title.

        364.36099433

Publisher: Fiona Schultz
Managing Editor: Martin Ford
Production controller: Grace Gutwein
Project Editor: Michael McGrath
Designer: Greg Lamont
Cover design and pic: Greg Lamont
Printer: Griffin Press, Adelaide, Australia
First published in Australia by Blake Publications 2004

CONTENTS

Apology
To Those Harmed in Queensland Institutions during their Childhood

We the government and churches together welcome the report of the Forde Commission of Inquiry into Abuse of Children in Queensland Institutions.

We acknowledge that there have been failures with respect to the children entrusted to our care, despite all the good the Institutions did in the light of their day. The result has been a system in which some children have suffered maltreatment, and their social, emotional, and physical needs have been neglected.

We sincerely apologise to all those people who suffered in any way while resident in our facilities, and express deep sorrow and regret at the hurt and distress suffered by those who were victims of abuse.

We accept the finding of the Forde Inquiry that government under-funding and consequent under-resourcing was a significant factor in the failure to provide adequate services to children in care.

We are committed to establishing and continuing dialogue with victims of abuse in institutions to discuss the basis for providing appropriate responses. We acknowledge that discussions are well advanced between some parties.

We are committed to working together with victims of abuse in institutions to ensure the provision of appropriately coordinated services through the establishment of a "one stop shop", as recommended by the Forde Inquiry. This initiative will be integrated with church and government run services and processes for bringing about reconciliation with victims of abuse in institutions. The focus will be on providing victims with the most effective path to healing. We are committed to continuing to provide such services as long as they are needed.

We recognise the value of formal reconciliation experiences in healing the hurt some have suffered, and undertake to plan these in consultation with former residents.

We are committed to doing all we reasonably can to ensure that children in our care are not subject to abuse and neglect. Further, we are committed to ongoing review and improvement of our services to children and families.

Peter Beattie MLA
Premier of Queensland

Anna Bligh MLA
Minister for Families, Youth and Community Care
Minister for Disability Services

The Most Reverend John Bathersby DD.
Catholic Archbishop of Brisbane

The Most Reverend Peter Hollingworth,
Anglican Archbishop of Brisbane

Reverend Dr David Pitman, Moderator,
Uniting Church in Australia (Qld Synod)

Hillmon Buckingham, Commissioner,
Territorial Commander, Australia Eastern Territory.
The Salvation Army

Bill Gynther, President,
Baptist Union of Queensland

Reverend Peter Overton, Conference President,
Churches of Christ in Queensland

FOREWORD

Although I have not had the pleasure to meet face-to-face with Al 'Crow' Fletcher, I consider it an honour to write the foreword to his memoirs of a mostly horrendous childhood. It is a worthy contribution to an emerging body of literature that offers insights into the vulnerabilities of those who as children experienced institutional care in Australia last century. What is unique about *Brutal: Surviving Westbrook Boys' Home* is its frank and relentless accounts of state 'care' that was unquestionably criminal in nature. That he and others survived the horrific events described in this book is a testament to their courage to make it through the toughest of times. That some did not is sickening. That those who inflicted such outrageous treatment on young vulnerable boys have escaped prosecution is outrageous. That those who did survive have not been compensated adequately is plain unjust.

Seven years have now passed since I first immersed myself in the experiences of those who, as children either spent time in or were raised in institutional care in Australia. I continue to still be absorbed by their stories and their pain. However, having read Crow's *Brutal*, my outrage at what many of Australia's citizens have endured as vulnerable children under the care of the state is again inflamed. It is a difficult read. There is little in Crow's account of time spent in Westbrook that does not shock; one wonders how such brutality and inhumanity could be visited on young boys. More to the point, how could the authorities allow it to continue after the 1961 Schwarten Inquiry revealed the terrible conditions and cruel treatment that were entrenched in the Brook's culture of harsh state 'care'.

My interest and absorption in these matters does have a private dimension. At the age of two, I was placed in a children's institution in England, from which I was shipped to Southern Rhodesia as a

Fairbridge child migrant at the age of 4. Many decades later, and after being elected to the Senate in 1996, child migrant organisations sought me out because of my personal history. They implored me to use my political influence to have their story exposed in federal parliament. After months of long and hard lobbying, and with the political support of the Australian Labor Party, the Senate Community Affairs References Committee Inquiry into child migration was established in 2000. As it turned out, the Inquiry's 2001 report was unanimous. *Lost Innocents: Righting the Record*, has done much to bring to light this invisible and sadly dark chapter of Australia's history.

During the child migrant inquiry, two submissions were received that shouted for another inquiry. One was from Mr Wayne Chamley of Broken Rites, the other from the Care Leavers of Australia Network (CLAN), pointing out that there were many thousands of other Australians who had been raised in care who also needed to be heard and acknowledged. The Aboriginal 'stolen generation' and child migrants had had their inquiries, when were other Australians – just like Crow – going to have their turn? Establishing another inquiry was once more a long and arduous task, but this time it was not opposed by the Coalition. Just as the child migrant report had, the 2004 report of this inquiry, *Forgotten Australians,* revealed yet another hidden and tragic chapter of Australian history.

Although I have been associated with literally hundreds of committee inquiries in nearly ten years as a Senator, nothing ever prepared me for, or compares with, the emotional experience of examining the tough issues around the vulnerabilities and often traumatic consequences of children being raised in care. To say that I, and all others involved, were often stressed is an understatement. Any party political differences between committee members quickly broke down because of the nature of the evidence. We heard stories that defied belief and stories that made us weep. Horrific accounts of criminal physical and sexual assault, of profound emotional abuse and neglect and of slave labour were common. Even more tragic were the sad stories of the loss of family, of siblings being torn apart, of the loss of identity and of an emptiness that has had a profound impact on their lives and on the lives of their partners and children.

It was during the child migrant inquiry that I first learnt of Westbrook, a Queensland state-run reformatory farm for boys between the ages of 10 and 18 years. I read a submission from a man who first experienced 'care' as a state ward at the infamous Neerkol orphanage. Having survived Neerkol's brand of abuse, he was happy to learn that he would be going to Westbrook, described to him as a 'nice farm'. What he encountered was horrifying. I recall thinking at the time what a hell-hole of a place it must have been. Certainly, there were other hell-holes, but some do stand out more than others because of their brutal regimes. Of his time in Westbrook, this man wrote:

'I was on a number of occasions viciously flogged till I bled, I could not take showers because if I did I would be attacked for sexual abuse, the screws (guards) were f…ing the boys, at will, and some of the older boys were standing over the younger ones, doing the same thing. At night I was afraid to sleep, I would hear boys taken out of the dormitory and then their screams and crying as they were being abused. I would eventually cry myself to sleep, night after night, exhausted by sheer terror' (Sub. 217).

More submissions were received from former Westbrook boys during the second inquiry. One wrote of his 'incarceration' in a similar way, adding that he was a survivor. "They may have beaten me, but they never managed to break me. Others were not so fortunate. Some of Australia's [worst] criminals are graduates of the Westbrook regime" (Sub. 141).

Crow's *Brutal* expands on these accounts. It is packed with shocking descriptions of the serious physical and psychological harm dished out continuously to the 'inmates'. I use the word inmates because they were treated as if they were actually the most dangerous or malicious of criminals, rather than the vulnerable kids they were. However, having said that, I could not ever condone the atrocious and heartless treatment meted out to the 'Brook' boys even being meted out to hardened criminals. Even though some of these boys had committed minor misdemeanours and were regarded as delinquents, most came from disadvantaged families where alcoholism, poverty and neglect were the norm. Like Crow, and as the *Forgotten Australians Report* reveals, many children found themselves in a court of law where they were ultimately charged with being a neglected child and sentenced to institutional care. In itself a frightening experience, but what lay ahead for many was far more terrifying. Already troubled children became victims of a system that merely compounded their trauma.

The following pages depict boys being subject to vicious floggings, to sexual assaults and to work routines that would test the fittest of men. They also reveal boys attempting suicide or 'suspiciously disappearing', boys finding the notorious Boggo Road Gaol for adult criminals a welcome relief from the 'Brook'. Additionally, they tell of how this boys' farm operated as a closed entity, where any abuse reported by the boys was disbelieved and resulted in further punishments. The harsh treatment was tolerated by management and occurred with little if any accountability or transparency. These appalling stories are partially tempered by the coping mechanisms the boys used to survive, such as several escape attempts and the camaraderie of other 'inmates' such as Schongie. His steadiness and strength, Crow writes, could be counted on when the going got really tough. To read of Schongie's ultimate fate is particularly heart-rending. The story of Boots Hobson is equally disturbing, as is the chapter of time spent in 'the compound' erected for recalcitrant boys. Crow poignantly writes of looking into other boys' faces and seeing that the boy had gone; that they looked like hardened men out of a concentration camp.

This reality of stolen childhoods, of childhood innocence being quickly replaced with a state of fear and a sense of alienation was a major finding of the two Senate inquiries. They also found that the culture of neglect and violence that these children survived has meant their adult lives have been littered with troubles. Although there were some good stories of people overcoming adversity through the love and support of others, the enduring legacy of child abuse can only described as disastrous. With few life skills and poor life chances, homelessness, unemployment, substance abuse, terms of imprisonment, relationship and mental health problems are all too common. And it does not end there. These effects can often be transferred on to the survivor's children, thus creating generational social problems that come at an enormous social and economic cost.

It is shameful that what occurred at Westbrook and a myriad of other institutions caring for children during the 20th century has largely just been accepted and ignored by politicians, by the legal system and by those organisations responsible for running orphanages and homes. Indeed, for all those who endured and suffered abuse while in care, their pleas for justice and for measures to amend have largely fallen on deaf ears. Token apologies may have been made, but these have not been accompanied by or followed up with meaningful acts of reparation and compensation. There has not been enough outrage as in Ireland where, in response to allegations of abuse in orphanages, industrial schools and other institutions, the Government agreed to introduce a compensatory scheme for victims of institutional abuse in 2001. Under the Residential Institutions Redress Act 2001, a no-fault scheme for compensation was established for people who had suffered sexual, physical or emotional abuse while in care. The scheme is primarily funded by the state, but the Catholic Church also provides monies for the compensation fund. For the most part, this scheme is viewed positively by the survivors of abuse. In Canada, several provincial governments and the federal government have established compensation schemes in response to situations where children were abused and neglected in state-funded and operated institutions.

In Australia, the Tasmanian Government recently introduced a compensation scheme for victims of abuse while in state care. Several churches and agencies also provide monetary compensation as part of their redress packages. However, there is no national scheme. The issue of monetary compensation is contentious. Some do not want any part of being paid-off for what they suffered and continue to endure, while others welcome some monies in their advancing years, especially after suffering social and economic disadvantage for many years. Considering that justice through the legal system is beyond reach for survivors of institutional abuse because of limitations law, to be compensated financially can acknowledge the injustices of the experiences suffered. To this end, Recommendation Six of the *Forgotten Australians Report* recommends that the Commonwealth Government establish and manage a national reparations fund for victims of institutional abuse. It suggests that such a "...scheme be funded by contributions from the Commonwealth and the State Governments and the Churches and agencies proportionately." Part of this fund's agenda would be to offer compensation for individuals who have been abused while in institutional and other forms of out-of-home care settings. It seems only just that such a scheme be established because the sheer scale of damaged people is staggering

Together with the 'stolen generation' inquiry, the child migrant and children in institutional inquiries reveal that upwards of and possibly more than 500 000 children were raised in institutional care in Australia last century. If we multiply this number by all those whose lives they have subsequently touched, there is likely millions of Australians who have been directly or indirectly affected by childhood trauma. It is vital that politicians and policymakers get to understand that if you harm a child you end up with a harmed adult. It is also vital that they get to understand that the flow-on effects are almost incalculable, that they not only impact on the individual survivors, but also on their families and society at large. Moreover, the costs translate into a massive drain on the public purse. For instance, a historic national report published by the Kids First Foundation in 2003 estimated that child abuse and neglect costs Australian taxpayers almost $5 billion a year.

It is critical that the political voice be increasingly motivated and heard when addressing issues relating to child abuse and trauma. It is critical that individuals and organisations break the barriers of ignorance. Once an understanding is achieved. Once politicians grasp that the huge social and economic costs of childhood trauma across a person's lifespan justify prevention, limitation and remedial measures, then we will get action. There is certainly sufficient research now available to justify action. The Senate child migrant and children in institutional care inquiries are but two of a long line of inquiries that date back many decades. Accordingly, the expectation would be that significant advances have occurred for children at risk. However, it is difficult to see where progress has been made, to see past children at risk being nothing more than objects requiring placement and social control. The question arises: how many inquiries and recommendations are required before action does take place?

It seems much more pressure is needed in view of the Federal Government's November 2005 Response to *Forgotten Australians* and *Protecting Vulnerable Children*. The latter being the second report of the 2004 institutional care inquiry, which covers foster care, young people with disabilities in care and children and young people in juvenile justice and detention centres.

Overall, it is an extremely disappointing response. Time and time again, the Coalition Government just refers the recommendations to the states and territories or to the churches and past providers of 'care' for institutionalised children. The expectation or hope that the Coalition Government would show commitment by assuming national leadership has not been realised.

Even more disappointing is the Government's general shrugging of the shoulders at what the survivors of institutional abuse suffered and continue to endure. Its refusal to even consider establishing a national reparations fund, as exists in Canada, Ireland and even Tasmania, indicates a hard-edged approach. The reign of terror described here by Crow occurred in too many institutions, resulting in thousands of suicides, many tens of thousands of sexual assaults, hundred of thousands of physical assaults and consequent trauma for many of the adults those children became. Sadly, the opportunity to make amends has not been taken up by this Government.

In fact, hardly anywhere in the Response is there any willingness by the Government to put its hand in its pocket. What a contrast to the way it splashes out with abandon on things that matter to it, such as the tens of millions of dollars expended on advertising workplace relations' reform. What is more, there is nothing in the Response that even goes close to matching the great energy and commitment the Government is currently investing in countering the threat of terrorism. Rightly so, however, we should remember that the terror inflicted on children also caused much death and injury.

It is not as if this terror has abated. Right across Australia an ever-increasing number of child abuse and neglect reports are being received by child protection authorities. As most of these departments are under-resourced, under-staffed or staffed by inexperienced people, many of these reports are never attended to and sadly result in the loss of life for some children.

I will continue to campaign and hope for the time when a Federal Government will lead the way in tackling the scourge of child abuse. It is a matter of national importance requiring a three-pronged national approach.

First, concerted research to measure the scale and costly lifespan effects of child abuse must be carried out.

Second, the Government must display the political will to translate this research into long-term policy reform that can make a real difference.

Third, and for optimal effect, these reforms need to be implemented as a coordinated national approach that is sufficiently funded with adequate resources. Although a difficult task, it is achievable.

All Australian children have the right to reach their full potential as productive and functional citizens.

They deserve nothing less.

The future wellbeing of Australian society depends on it.

Senator Andrew Murray
Senator for Western Australia
Australian Democrats
November 2005

PROLOGUE

By degrees we beheld the infinite Abyss.
WILLIAM BLAKE

The thought of that place was almost too much for me to bear. Not that I had any exact idea of what I was in for yet, but you heard of blokes comin' back from there different from when they went in. I had heard that they did terrible things to you in there.

I'd been sentenced to Westbrook 'until eighteen years old or otherwise dealt with'. That was two and a half years! I tried to think back two and a half years to get an idea of how long that'd be. But it was impossible. It seemed like forever. I might just as well have been sentenced 'for the term of his natural life'.

It was the 25th June 1960. I'll never forget that date. Suddenly things were very serious. I'd been picked up by the cops from the Brisbane Airport and taken to the Brisbane watch-house where I had to spend the night.

There was another boy in there with me, a quiet, redheaded kid. He didn't look so great. His hair stood up like he was seein' a ghost, his eyes kept darting about and the freckles on his face stood out like big black threepenny bits on his white skin.

The floor of the cell was damp. There was a bunk against the wall and a toilet in the corner. The bunk stank of vomit. The redhead pointed to it and said, 'Mind if I have this for a while? I don't feel too good.'

'Lie on it all you like, mate,' I said, 'if it'll make you feel any better.'

There was a couple of blankets on the bunk and they stank of vomit too. I folded one of them and put it on the floor to sit on, movin' as far away from the toilet and the boy on the bunk as I could get. He'd just laid down and seemed to pass out. He was snorin' softly. I was amazed that someone could just go to sleep like that in a place like this.

My head was spinnin'. I was close to screamin'. Him being so quiet probably helped me keep myself together. I sat on the floor and watched him.

The thought occurred to me that maybe he really was crook and needed a doctor. I wondered if I should yell out for someone to come, but decided against it. Better not to make too many waves till I sussed the situation out a bit. Not that I was capable of much clear thought then. So I just squatted on the floor, tryin' not to touch anything, listenin' to him breathin'.

I drew my knees up and huddled in the corner. 'How the hell did I get myself into this mess?' I kept askin' myself.

Queensland's first boys' reformatory was established
on the prison hulk *The Proserpine* in 1871.

In 1881, the boys were transferred from the hulk to some buildings at Lytton.

In 1900, 88 boys and some of the buildings were transferred
to Westbrook, near Toowoomba.

This new institution was called
The Reformatory for Boys, Westbrook.

EARLY DAYS

Children were placed in homes for many reasons: families in crisis, poverty, death of a parent, mental illness and family breakdown. Families in these situations had few services to draw on and little financial assistance from government. The attitudes of the day also worked against some families staying together, as fathers were not seen as appropriate caregivers while single unmarried mothers experienced significant social stigma.

Some families in crisis chose to send their children to homes rather than risk welfare intervention. Other children were placed in care because they were seen as being out of control and in need of supervision and training. Many children were not told why they were being placed in care, while for others the poverty, neglect and violence were all too easily remembered.

Forgotten Australians
Senate Committee Report on Australians who experienced institutional
or out-of-home care as children. 2004

So where did this all start?

I suppose, in Peel Street, South Brisbane. That was the first place I remember livin'. My Nanna had a boarding house there. We probably had lots of people living there at different times. I remember, apart from my mother and father and my two sisters, Maree and Denise, there was a bloke called Harry livin' there. Like Dad, he was just back in Brisbane from the war.

Harry used to get these terrible headaches. I can remember him singin' out and swearin' in his sleep. It used to scare me, mind you I was only two or three years old at the time. One night when he was drunk, he went to bed holdin' a cigarette in his hand and he accidentally set the place on fire. Luckily Mum and Nanna were able to put it out before everything went up in smoke.

But he was a good friend to me, was Harry. He made me this wonderful rockin' horse and used to play games with me when I was a little bloke. Then one day he was just gone. Years later Nanna told me that the war had sent him insane and he had got sent to the funny farm.

Dad was a good mate in them days too and I loved him. He was a Merchant Seaman and used to go away a lot. Apparently when he was away I used to ask Mum and Nanna every day when he would be back. Durin' the war he rose to the rank of First Officer. He was on the Liberty ships. They had a terrible reputation. See the Liberty ships were put together in a real hurry, so they were pretty rough. Some of them broke up in the storms. Dad did six safe trips across the Atlantic before they got torpedoed on the seventh. More than half the crew lost their lives then. Durin' the war they lost a lot of merchant ships and a lot of merchant seamen.

Yair, and while I remember it. Dad had a real lot of American medals, and I mean a lot. He give them all to me to play with. Denise and me used to make mud pies and use them for decorations. Dad didn't care. I suppose that's what he really thought of war.

There was a lot of Yanks in South Brisbane in them days, mostly Negro servicemen who were stationed over there durin' the war and stayed for a few years after. I can remember one day a wheel comin' off a jeep and rollin' down the hill and me chasin' it and rollin' it back to where the soldiers were waitin'. They put their hands in their pockets and give me a pile of coins. Nanna was pretty pleased 'cause I gave them all to her. We had a few treats for tea that night.

Nanna was only about five foot tall. She may have been little but she was a strong-lookin' lady. She had a strong faith in God too, though she didn't go to no church. She was an honorary member of the Seamen's Union of Australia, which was unusual for a woman, and she was a close friend of Elliot who was the head man of the Union down in Sydney.

So after the war, Dad kept on signin' the articles to go to sea. But only as an Able Bodied Seaman, he was never again on the bridge of a ship. He'd started gettin' into bad ways with his drinkin' and violence. Nanna told me once that durin' the war he accidentally stabbed his best mate in the neck with a boathook. They were tryin' to get a lifeboat clear just after they was torpedoed. Well, you can imagine it, can't you? Here they are tryin' to push the boat off with the hook and they've got to support the body of the bloke who was caught on it at the same time. Johnno died in Dad's arms. They had to put him over the side. That used to prey on Dad's mind a lot, Nanna said, and he probably drank to blot out the memory of it. But then, she always made excuses for him.

But we were always so happy when Dad first got home from sea. We'd unpack his kitbag to get all the goodies he'd brought back for us. There was lots of tinned food and biscuits and maybe it'd once been part of the ship's cargo, we didn't care. But then he'd go down the pub with his mates—The Queens Hotel, The Port Office and The National.

Next mornin' it was 'Al, go to the shop. One bottle of Tonic Water and one Bex.'

Poor Mum, she couldn't change him. He was a tough, strong man see. And she had her own problems. Before she met Dad she was set to marry a U.S. naval officer who had been highly decorated, only he got killed at Pearl Harbour.

She was a beautiful-lookin' woman, Mum, fairly reserved, I suppose. But practically everyone that knew her seemed to have a good word for her.

When Dad was at home, he used to play football for South Brisbane. He was the vice captain and his photo is in Souths Footy Club. 'Speedy Louie', they used to call him, or 'Louie the Lug'. But the grog was gettin' to him. When he was home for any period of time, all he wanted was the pub and his drinkin' mates. He forgot all about us, his family. I was the one he sent down to hail a cab every morning. Then he'd be off, usually to the Port Office Hotel. In the afternoon he'd be back, with six bottles.

He also gave up playin' cricket in the street with me like he did when

I was smaller. He'd rather go into the house and listen to it on the radio.

Then when the money ran out, it was off to sign the articles and back to sea again.

Mum got fed up. She found a place for us to live at Ekibin. During the war there had been a big supply dump there and there was all these Nissen huts made of corrugated iron that looked like big metal tubes that somebody had cut in half. They looked like igloos and that's what a lot of people called them. Families who had nowhere else to go after the war lived in them.

It was a dreary place, that. There were no trees or gardens, just earth around the huts, which became mud in rainy weather. I don't remember much laughter there, but I suppose Mum thought it was better than Peel Street. Everyone lived close together and the children there went barefoot and were mostly dressed in rags. We had a copper boiler for the laundry and a forty-four gallon drum cut in half for washin' ourselves.

Dad came home from sea and lived with us there and for a while things seemed to go all right. Then he and Mum started their fightin' again. They were both so strong-willed, see. Neither of 'em would give in.

Early one morning Mum left. Me and my sisters pleaded with her not to go, but she'd had enough. Dad just said 'Good riddance' to her, but he was still drunk, so what did he care? Mum was cryin' and she said she'd come back for us sometime.

Us three kids were howlin' our eyes out when Dad's mates turned up. Some of the neighbours said they'd take the girls and look after them, but Dad insisted that I stayed with him. I'll always remember that day when Mum left. I asked Dad when she would be home again. He said that he didn't think she'd be comin' back at all. I screamed at him, 'I want my Mum!'

'Shut up and act your age!' he said. I think I was about six at the time.

I finished up crawlin' under the igloo, though it was only about a foot off the ground. Dad's mates and some of our neighbours tried to get me to come out but I stayed there most of the day, just cryin' for my mother. When it got dark I crawled back out. I was covered in mud from my own tears.

Dad filled the oil drum with water and gave me a good clean up. There was food on the table for me but I didn't want it, so he locked me in one of the rooms. 'He'll be all right in the morning,' he said. Him and his mates were really pissed by then.

But next morning I wasn't all right. When he let me out of the room I started cryin' again for Mum and my sisters. He started bellowin' at me and before I knew it, I was under that hut again.

By this time the neighbours were startin' to get concerned. They called a doctor who advised them to get my grandmother. So Dad went back to Peel Street to get Nanna. When I saw her, I did come out, but I hung on to her tight and I wouldn't let her go.

However before the day was over, Mum was back. My sisters and I were happy but things weren't the same no more. Dad tried to behave himself but I was scared of him now and so was Mum.

A few weeks later he signed articles on another ship. We all gave him big hugs as if nothing had happened. He seemed to be gone a long time, though, this time. It might have been nine months or even a year.

During his absence Mum managed to get us a Housing Commission home at Holland Park. It was a brand new house on the corner of a street and we had everything we wanted there. We had our own rooms and plenty of toys.

Then Dad came back from sea. All was well for a little while until him and Mum started fightin' again. He was drunk all the time. Nobody could put up with him. He was a fair bastard.

At this time there was a lady who lived nearby who owned about three or four picture theatres in the city. She was a very wealthy woman and she took a likin' to me. She asked my mother to let me come and live with her.

I think me mother would have agreed, for my sake. Mum could see this woman could have given me a good life. I reckon this lady also had a fair idea of what was goin' on at home with me father drunk all the time. But anyhow, Nanna wouldn't have it.

This lady bought a house opposite the school I attended so she could see me at lunchtime. She would have a hot lunch ready for me every school day and afternoon tea for after school. She wanted to feed me and look after me. It was probably this lady who bought all the furniture and toys in that house for us. Mum wouldn't have been able to. But Nanna was against me goin' to live with her. She prevented it. After we moved from there, I never saw that kind lady again, in me life.

Anyway Dad was drinkin' worse and worse and rowin' with everyone. I remember during one of his fights with Mum that I ran away from the house. I went missin'. I climbed into an old well at the top of a road in some bushland. I suppose I was tryin' to get away from the fightin'.

The neighbours went searchin' for me and the police were called in. When they did locate me they had to call the fire brigade to get me out of the well.

Apparently this well was a very dangerous place. It was full of snakes and spiders, as well as dirty water. I was lucky they found me and got me out alive.

The next part of the story might have had something to do with that rich lady because one day Mum told my sisters and me that she had a plan for us. We would go and stay at a lovely place called 'Silky Oaks' out near Wynnum. This was a Home for children. We would stay there until she could get a nice place for us all to live together again.

Mum's idea to get us into a Home was really about gettin' us away from my father and Nanna, though of course she didn't tell us this. She would be payin' one pound ten a week to keep us there while she was workin' full-time to get enough money for another place for us.

Maree went first and then Denise. Finally I was taken out there too. We were driven out in a car with a dickey seat, can't remember whose it was.

I thought about Nanna and Dad. I was worried about them. For of course, they weren't even mentioned in the plan.

SILKY OAKS 'Haven for Children'

He ([Edwin Smith) pleaded guilty ... to a series of counts involving former Silky Oaks residents...

The events concerning Smith raise a number of issues about the standard of care provided for the child at Silky Oaks between 1960 and 1965. First is the question of how a person such as Smith could have been placed in a position of responsibility and trust with unlimited opportunity for the abuse of the children under his control.

Commission of Inquiry into Abuse of Children in Queensland Institutions
Leneen Forde AC, 1999.

I always remember Silky Oaks as *The Lolly Farm.* I don't remember anything particularly bad about the place, but Maree and Denise say different. The stories they told me about what happened to them are wicked. It has taken the Forde Inquiry to bring it all out, nearly half a century later. It revealed that even the superintendent of that home was a pedophile.

Anyway, that's me sisters' and other people's business, so I won't go into it.

I got there on a Sunday and was taken in and shown my bed straight away. It was in a long dormitory with a polished wooden floor, boys on one side, girls on the other. The beds were very close together. The grounds were quite large though and there was a beautiful view of the sea.

I couldn't find the words to explain the dreadful feeling of loss when Mum left me there. I was cryin' and and beggin' her not to go and she was tellin' me that she would come back and get us when she had a nice place for us to stay, but that didn't make it any easier. Obviously Mum had to put us in the home for a while. It would have been real rough on her too.

Then about 3.00pm that day, the children were all called to gather at the front of the building. Everyone was smiling as if Santa Claus was comin'. Someone sang out 'Here he comes! Ooh! It's the Lolly Man!'

The Lolly Man was the highlight of the week. He came every Sunday afternoon. He stood on the verandah and threw lollies among us kids. Everyone was scrabblin' like chooks to get their rewards.

I went to sleep that night to the sounds of lots of children tryin' to settle down in the semi-darkness. Some were singin' out, some were cryin'. It was always like that, depressin'. Unwanted children in an unwanted place.

Morning came and it was time to get up and get ready for school, Manly State School it was. We walked there along a dirt road mostly through bushland. You could see the blue of the sea through the trees and Stradbroke Island way off on the horizon.

The school was small and it had a nice atmosphere. The 'Outsiders' and the 'Home' kids seemed to get on with each other okay. I done well there and it was only a little while after I arrived there that they put me up a grade.

In the garden of the Lolly Farm, there was a frangipani tree. My sisters and me had sat under it when we said goodbye to Mum. Sunday was visiting day, so we used to sit under that frangipani tree and wait for Mum, but she didn't come for a long while. We were the only ones sittin' there. Most of the children there were State Wards and as such didn't get no visitors, but we believed that Mum would come and get us. One day.

Weeks went by and there was still no visit from Mum. We still used to sit under the tree on Sundays, but after a while we never stayed there for very long. Nobody explained to us what was goin' on, so we got to expectin' to be disappointed.

Then out of the blue Nanna and Dad arrived. They said that they had got a beautiful home for us all to live in. Denise and I packed our things and said goodbye to the others. We were pretty excited. I don't know where Maree was. She didn't sleep in the same dormitory as Denise and me.

We climbed into the back of a big car.

'What about Maree?'

'She can't come with us today,' said Dad. 'We might be able to come and get her later on.'

We drove off down the road to Brisbane and after what seemed a long time, we finally pulled into the driveway of a house.

'This is it,' said Dad, 'our new home.'

It was beautiful. Everything smelled fresh. There wasn't much furniture, but it looked good to us.

After a few months Maree turned up. I don't know how that happened, one day she was just there.

We must have gone to school, but I can't remember it. I don't even know how long we lived there in that new place, because it didn't seem very long after, that one day we were all back at the Lolly Farm again. I can't remember how that happened, either. We were just back there and took up where we left off.

My schoolin' went downhill.

They tried all kinds of things to help me at school, one teacher even gave me sixpence every week when I was good. That was a lot of money to a kid in them days.

I behaved, but I had a plan. I was goin' to get out of this place. It was my first escape. It happened one Sunday afternoon after the lolly man had been and gone.

I had some bread and some lollies saved for this big day. Denise gave me her lollies, but she was too scared to come with me.

It was quite late when I slipped away and started walkin' towards Brisbane. Every time I seen a car or people comin' I hid. I kept walkin' till well after dark. It got pretty cold and I started gettin' scared, especially when I sat down in some bushes at the side of the road. Something moved in the scrub behind me, probably an animal of some sort. I got really frightened and ran back to the Lolly Farm and I sat under the frangipani tree and ate some of me bread and lollies.

That's where they found me. I got whacked, given a cold shower and put to bed. My bag of lollies was confiscated, of course.

No more pennies for me at school now. From then on everyone left me alone.

I couldn't have cared less.

Silky Oaks was now our home. We became like the State Ward kids. We didn't get no visitors, we just did whatever the other kids did. I suppose we behaved ourselves. I can't remember anything good happenin' or ever lookin' forward to anything. We just lived there.

Then one day Nanna and Dad arrived. Mum was there too. I remember Mum was cryin' and sayin' that Denise and me could go and live with Nanna and Dad, but Maree couldn't. It was the law she said.

Dad said they had got another real nice house for us to live in.

This time I wasn't very impressed. Denise was very excited, but I was feelin' suspicious.

Nevertheless we packed our things and said goodbye to our friends again. It was very sad to see the hurt in their faces. We were free and they had to stay.

I suppose they had the Lolly Man to look forward to.

We got in the car. I turned and stared out the back window. I saw Mum and Maree walkin' back towards the dormitory.

As we drove along the road back to Brisbane, I tried to pick out the places where I had hidden by the roadside, but everything looked completely different from the car. Maybe we were even goin' in the opposite direction.

Nanna was chatterin' on about this beautiful old colonial home they had bought on three-quarters of an acre. Ampol had bought out her lease on the boardin' house at Peel Street and she had put the money for a deposit on this new place. It cost seven hundred and fifty pounds. Dad got a war service loan for it, which Nanna organised for him. If it wasn't for Nanna, I reckon we would have been in Homes all our lives.

But now I was thinkin' of Maree and had to fight back the tears. I was in two minds about everything.

It was after dark when we got to our new home, which was at

Enoggera, on the north side of Brisbane. It was a high-set house, a real old Queenslander in top condition, and it was big, on what seemed to be a huge block. There were large gums and other trees in the yard. Everybody seemed real happy so I cheered up when I saw it too.

I had a bed, or a mattress, on the floor and a little wardrobe on the verandah. Denise slept at the other end of the verandah. Nanna's bedroom was in the middle of the house and Dad's was at the front. We had a big kitchen with a wood stove and a bathroom with a chip heater. We put newspaper and wood chips into the heater and got the flames roarin' away for a hot bath.

Under the house there was a laundry with three washtubs where Nanna could soak the clothes and wash them by hand. There was a set of hand wringers too. The linen and stuff like that went into a big copper boiler.

In the kitchen we had an icebox, a radio and a table with four chairs. We felt so lucky.

But for the first few days it was hard for Denise and me to get used to the quiet. At the Lolly Farm there was always some kids cryin' themselves to sleep, or kids singin' out with bad dreams, or something like that. It was a restless place, that dormitory.

Eventually we settled in. Dad was good to us. Except that Mum wasn't there, it seemed like a normal family. We walked to school barefoot like most of the other kids. We were free.

Dad took a job on the tugs in Brisbane. For about a year he seemed content, but then his itchy feet took him away from us, back to sea. Sometimes he was away for months, but then sometimes only weeks. It was so great when he came home. We'd unpack his kitbag and get the goodies that seamen and wharfies bring back for their families. He always brought beer with him too, which Nanna didn't mind. She wouldn't have plonk in the house, though.

Dad would also bring his mates home with him, but in those days they behaved like gentlemen, especially Ronnie Roberts who always stayed with us when he was ashore in Brisbane. And then there was Bobby Kirby who helped Dad paint the house bright red and brilliant yellow with funnel paint, compliments of the Australian National Line, of course. Dunno what the neighbours thought.

Nanna, me and Denise worked very hard in the yard. We built a chook pen for Nanna's chooks and old Diddy the duck. I made a big vegetable garden, there was plenty of good fertiliser, which we got straight from the thunderbox. I grew lettuce, silver beet and other vegies. I used to go round the neighbourhood after school sellin' them. I'd get sixpence for a good lettuce but not much for silverbeet. The tomatoes I grew for ourselves, only because people didn't understand the value of them in them days. I sometimes made a couple of quid a week, which I gave straight to Nanna.

Our life then was pretty good, even though we were poor people in that neighbourhood. We might have had that big house but there wasn't much money around then. Most people had vegie gardens and chooks to keep 'em goin'. We never seen grubs or vermin around the yard because the chooks'd clean them up because we'd always let 'em out for at least a couple of hours a day. We didn't need no poisons. Nature was more in balance then, than it is today.

If I wasn't sellin' many vegies, I used to go down to Tom Gurney's dairy farm with six sugar bags and pick up some cow manure to make some extra money. When I had a bagful, I'd put it in the wheelbarrow and push it bit by bit up the hill. I sold most of it to an Indian man for his rose garden, but he was hard with money. A shilling a bag he gave me. I could pick up two a day. Sometimes I used to get a gallon of milk off old Tom for two bob, straight from the cow. I took it home for Nanna, plus any money I had left over.

It was Nanna's birthday in September. I worked extra hard to buy a present for her from Denise and me. We got her this beautiful round vase with a lid on it for eight and sixpence. Top quality china, it was. Nanna was thrilled.

Then Nanna decided I should join the Boy Scouts. She got Denise into the Red Cross. I didn't like Scouts much, there were too many stuck-up people there, so I left. Couldn't afford it, anyway. I didn't care. I had better things to do. Denise stayed in the Red Cross but, for a long time. She looked great in her white uniform and red cardigan.

So next, Nanna gets me into the YMCA in the city, next door to the People's Palace, which is the Salvation Army place across the road from Central Station. Every Saturday I used to go into town on one of them smoky old trains.

I loved it. I joined the hockey team. Our colours were red and white, same as Denise's. We used to play at the back of the Brisbane Hospital. For about six weeks I couldn't get a game, I was just a reserve. Then my big chance came. I played left forward and scored two goals. After that I was on the team permanent and got voted the team leader.

We kept winnin' and Ronnie Roberts bought me a good hockey stick. We won the premiership that year.

I was thinkin' Dad would be pretty proud of me because our wins used to be reported in the paper. He was on the old medical and troop ship, the *Bulolo*, runnin' from Sydney to Port Morseby at this time. He'd save the papers when they had my name in them for gettin' goals.

Dad came home and told us some bad news. Our good friend Ronnie Roberts had fallen off a wharf in Bundaberg, never to be seen again. The story went round that he'd had a few too many. They reckon a grouper got him, but I've thought about it a lot since and I reckon that he committed suicide because he had some trouble with his family. They never found his body, though.

It was a sad time for us for a long while. Plus, Ron always used to send money to Nanna, which used to help us out a bit. He adored her.

Now the money was really hard to get. Dad was at home with no work in Brisbane. There was easily a hundred men on the roster waiting for a ship. Frustration was buildin' up in him and he started drinkin' worse and worse. His mates used to give him money if they didn't shout him at the pub. He always seemed to have enough money for alcohol.

On Saturdays I used to get picked up in a ute to go and play hockey. Round about this time I put in my best performance. I scored six goals, but Dad wasn't the slightest bit impressed. Football and hockey are two totally different games and he used to tell me about football strategies which didn't make no sense in a game of hockey. We had an argument and he went berserk and smashed my hockey stick. I think he used to take his worries out on me.

Nanna was away at this time. She had gone away for a few weeks on doctor's orders. Without her, our house of happiness was turning into a house from hell.

The next Saturday the ute came round to pick me up. All the other kids were in the back, waitin' for me. As soon as I seen them comin', I shot out the back door and down to the creek. For a few Saturdays after that, the team used to come round to the house to try to find out why I wasn't comin' to play no more. I just bolted when they came. I never played hockey again, or any other sport for that matter, and I never went back to the YMCA.

I was about twelve years old at this time and startin' to stand up to Dad, but when he had a skinful, he had a very short fuse. He used to fly off the handle over any little thing and I was always the punchin' bag. Oh, he was sorry for what he'd done when he was sober, but he'd get pissed again and it would be the same old thing over and over again. I was sick of havin' black eyes.

When Nanna got back, Dad left the next day. He told her that he had to get onto the Sydney roster because there wasn't goin' to be any work out of Brisbane.

Saturday came and Denise got ready for Red Cross. Nanna sang out to me to get ready for hockey. I was outside seein' to the chooks and my new mate Billy the goat and a stray dog we had picked up, called Tinker. I sang out back to her, 'Not goin' no more!'

Nanna was dumbfounded. Though Denise said nothing at the time, later she told Nanna what had happened to my hockey stick. Nanna never mentioned hockey again.

One night, to everyone's shock and surprise, Mum arrived with Maree. Cryin', the girls and Mum hugged each other. Me, I could only hug Maree. I totally ignored Mum. Denise was Dad's girl, but I was special to Nanna. I just felt I couldn't go against Nanna and show love to Mum. My parents had christened me Alfred, but Nanna had always called me Alan. It was a special name to her because it was the name of a son she lost. So

I kept that name to please her.

After about an hour Mum and Maree left again. Maree told me that she would come to stay with us for a weekend sometimes, which she did.

It was about this time that I started to get sick all the while. It was probably nerves, I don't know, but I was often at the doctor's or up the hospital.

Mum sent me a nice shirt for my birthday that year. When I unwrapped it, Nanna said, 'You don't have to wear this, rip it up.'

I cried as I ripped up that thoughtful present. Nanna said it would get the hurt out of me, but I don't think it ever did.

To give Dad his credit, he never said anything bad about Mum to us kids. But I reckon he never really got over her, either. When he died, they found a photo of Mum in his pocket. They reckon Mum always had a photograph of him, too.

Slowly my life was changin'. For a start, I never went to school much no more. There didn't seem to be any point.

One day I was waggin' it at the big creek not far from our place and I met a guy called Peter who had a horse called Pancho. Peter was about twenty to twenty-five years old and he had a disability. He was related to Senator George Georges and lived on his chicken farm a few miles away in Bunyaville. Peter didn't have no friends because of his disability and the funny way he looked, so I became his best mate.

Nanna thought I was at school each day during school term and Denise never said nothin' to her about me waggin' it. Occasionally she would wag it with me, but I didn't want her gettin' into trouble so I always warned her not to turn out like me. Not that she ever went to school much, herself.

So no more school for me and no more cow shit, neither, but I always cleaned the yard and I did all the jobs Nanna set out for me to do each day.

See, Nanna had to get up real early to get to work at the Golden Circle cannery. She used to put our school lunches on the kitchen table for us before she left and relied on us to get ourselves to school and home again. You can't blame her for not knowin' that I was waggin' it.

She left home at five o'clock in the morning and used to get home on dark, or well after it in the winter, and if all our jobs were done she thought everything was okay.

When Peter couldn't leave the farm because George Georges wanted him there, he'd leave Pancho tied up at a certain place with a couple of dozen eggs for me to sell. George Georges never knew. I would ride Pancho and take in the wonders of such freedom. Nobody to answer to. I would sell the eggs so that I had some money to take home to Nanna. I always gave my lunch to Pancho. When I had spare money, I used to go to the shop and buy my favourite food, a bottle of milk and a packet of Monte Carlo biscuits.

I met some Aborigines who lived in a tin hut in Bunya when I was out ridin' Pancho. Bunya was practically all bush and a few miles from home. These people accepted me and asked me no questions; they became like a beautiful lovin' family to me. When I went to their place I always tried to take something for 'em, a couple of dozen eggs or a chook or two.

But they were treated like outcasts. They were looked down on because they were poor and black. Anyhow, they taught me a lot and I'll never forget their kindness to me. They eventually moved away from there. Their white neighbours drove them off.

One day when they were on the nellie, (plonk) I asked for a drink. They told me that it was poison. 'Brother, don't you ever touch it,' they said.

Life was better with them than it was at home. I joined in their singin' and strange dances and listened to the didgeridoo. I often stayed the night with them, turnin' up on a Friday with six chooks in a sugar bag and plenty of eggs pinched from George Georges' farm. Nanna thought I was stayin' with a schoolfriend.

We all slept on the dirt floor with blankets underneath and they always made sure that I was warm and comfortable. I had a crush on a girl in their family. She was called Banje. She was twelve or thirteen years old like me and very pretty. They all knew that I was sweet on her and used to laugh about it. The last time I stayed there she slept beside me.

Her beautiful warm body smelled like all the flowers of the bush.

Later in life I was to find out the hard way what most people thought about a white boy living with blackfellas.

To earn some more money, I got a cart for Billy the Goat and used to take little kids for rides on the weekends. I did pretty well out of it. I used to charge threepence or sixpence, whatever I could get, and once again took the money home to Nanna.

Times were gettin' bad for us. Dad still had no work and there was a lot of seamen waitin' on the rosters in Sydney and Brisbane. Dad decided to wait it out in Brisbane.

One day when I was waggin' it, two coppers called Jones and Flesser, who used to run around in a motorbike and sidecar, pulled me up. They said they had their eye on me, 'Get back to school,' one of 'em said.

'Yes sir.'

I went back. But I had been waggin' it for months and the Principal wouldn't have me. The only way out for me was a transfer.

My next school was Newmarket. I went there for two or three weeks and then got transferred to Kelvin Grove, but I couldn't stick it there either and started waggin' again.

The coppers got onto me and I got another transfer, this time to Michelton.

None of the schools really wanted me because they reckoned I was a bad influence. I lasted all of twenty minutes at Mitchelton! The headmaster told me he didn't want me there.

The coppers grabbed me the same day and wanted to know why I wasn't at school at Mitchelton. There was only one school left to try and that was Grovely. They drove me there and took me to the office. I got enrolled and then they took me home and told Nanna. They'd worked out that I had wagged it for nearly a whole year. Nanna was shocked. My father's comment was 'Well what would you expect from a shithouse rat?'

Nanna was told that if I kept waggin' school I would be charged with bein' a neglected child and finish up in Westbrook. She and Dad had to come up with a plan for me, so they came up with a brilliant one, they would pay for me to go to Riverview Salvation Army Home for Boys.

They both meant the best for me. They reckoned that if I went there for twelve months it would straighten me out. But as it turned out, there were no vacancies, so their plan had to be put on hold for a while.

Like a lot of other kids in that neighbourhood, I had been stealin' the occasional chook or one or two eggs and the fruit off trees and sometimes a bit of milk money. I had also been stealin' from the local bakery. The bread-carters used to hang their moneybags up in a room at the back. The office staff used to come in later and count the cash. I found a way to get my arm through the louvre windows and pinch a bit out of two or three of the bags. That way I always had money for me smokes and the pictures.

I had also made some new friends in the district and we thought up a way to rob an electrical store. We nicked some radios through the skylight usin' fishin' line and a grapplin' hook, then sold them cheap and split the proceeds.

The coppers were onto us and no mistake. They grabbed me again for waggin' school. But then Nanna got sick and because none of the schools wanted me, I was given a special permit to stay home and look after her. This meant the coppers couldn't nab me for waggin' it any more.

But by now me mates and me was marked. The coppers promised me that the first mistake I made, I'd land in Westbrook. The very mention of that name put shivers down me back.

One day we found a couple of boxes of rotten tomatoes. We took them down to a cutting in the railway line and took up positions on either side of it. In those days the trains were packed in the mornings and the windows were always down because of the heat. We knew that the train couldn't stop and nobody would jump out and grab us. When the train came through we let rip. Everyone got a tomato or part thereof, compliments of us.

I don't know to this day what made us do that. We should have got a swift kick up the arse for it, the lot of us. The coppers probably had a fair idea of who done it, but we got away with it.

Dad never let up on me. I remember one day Denise and me were fightin' while he was havin' a bath. He yelled out 'I'll kill you Alfred!' I told him to get stuffed, knowing full well the consequences of sayin' that. He let out a terrible roar and a stream of language you would have heard a mile away, he must've had a bad hangover. I locked him in the bathroom just in time and bolted. As I flew out of the house I heard him kickin' the door down.

He was in his underpants and had soap all over him and I had a good start on him, but he chased me through the streets all the way down to the creek. Thank God he never got me that day. Still, I knew what was goin' to happen when I got home and I was terrified. I came home after dark and sneaked into my bed on the verandah without makin' a sound.

But suddenly he was beside me screamin', 'You shithouse rat! You bodgie!'

He started bashin' me and just wouldn't stop. Finally he let up and went to bed. Bastard! I had two black eyes and me lips were split. My ribs were achin' something shockin'. I was a mess.

In the morning I couldn't move. He didn't even come in to see me, just told Denise to go next door and ring for a taxi to the Queens Hotel.

'Thank God he's gone', I thought.

My mate Joey came to see me. He was older than me, about seventeen. He took me home to his mother's place and she looked after me for about a week. Most of that time I stayed in bed, still sick and sore.

When I finally got back home, I found me pushbike hacked to pieces. That bike had belonged to my cousin Margaret who had died of leukemia at the age of seventeen. It had meant a lot to me, that bike. Dad had chopped it up with an axe and put the pieces on my bed. He was inside drinkin' with his mates.

When I seen the state of me bike, I went outside and got a big rock and put it right through his window. I scared the shit out of them bastards. I could hear them cursin' and scramblin' onto the verandah. Maybe they thought they'd been torpedoed again.

I waited under the back stairs and when Dad came down, wobblin' drunk and mutterin', 'I'll kill those bodgies!', I sneaked up behind him and hit him hard as I could with Nanna's wooden peg box. I got him a beauty. He staggered and fell to his knees. Then I bolted.

I don't know where Nanna was during all this, probably workin'. She wouldn't have allowed any of this to go on if she'd been present.

It got so bad that I couldn't go home unless my father was out or asleep, drunk as a skunk. Sometimes I stopped out all night and only came home when Nanna had gone to work and he had gone off in his taxi.

People kept right out of our business. I think the neighbours was too scared, worried about puttin' their noses into somethin' that wasn't their concern. There were a lot of tough men comin' to our house all the time. Seamen. They brought loads of piss and sometimes they brought their women with them. They got drunk and they got noisy.

Anyway, after I got back from Joey's place, Nanna had moved out on doctor's orders. She just couldn't take no more.

I got fed up with sneakin' about. Joey had a .22 repeater rifle so I borrowed it off him. I took it into bed with me and hid it under the blankets. If Dad was going to bash me, well I was going to give him a bullet in each leg. Not enough to kill him but, but enough to hurt him real bad. I planned it, cold-blooded.

He never came in the night I took that rifle to bed and to this day I'll never know why.

It was the longest night of my life. As I lay there, my thoughts became scattered in my brain. I might have dozed a bit, but it seemed to me that I was awake all night.

In the morning Joey turned up, very excited. 'Give me the rifle back right now,' he said. 'And the bullets.' His mother had put two and two together.

So then me and my mates Robin Parnell, Billy Campbell and Graham Cannon, we made this cubby house. We made it in the back-yard, which was very big, with lots of trees and shrubbery around. We dug out a huge hole about five feet by ten feet and about five feet deep and lined the walls with tin. We put in a timber floor and then roofed the whole thing over with tin and covered that with about a foot of soil.

There was a small entrance at the back. We had a little metho stove and a lantern inside. We dug trenches all around and covered them with sticks and leaves so that anyone sneakin' up would give themselves away.

Then we made a pledge to stick together, always, no matter what.

We were comin' back from the pictures one night, havin' a bit of a meetin' and we decided to get even. So we goes round to my place about midnight and we're armed with about fifty rocks. Two of us are in the front yard and two round the back. Then we let fly at the roof. The noise was terrific. Dad and his mates would have wondered what hit them. Probably thought it was a Jap Kamikaze attack.

But anyway, whatever they thought, we were gone.

Denise told me that they knew we done it and were goin' down the pub to get a few extra men and bash the lot of us, but it never happened.

Now I was sleepin' in the dugout when I was home.

A few days after the bombardment, I seen my Dad a fair way off, pissin' off the back steps. He yelled out, 'I'll kill you and your bodgie mates! You are not to eat food in this house no more. Ever!'

'Arsehole!' I sang out to him. 'Tell all your mates to be on guard, not to sleep too sound, because you aint seen nothin' yet! I'm going to get you bastards with petrol bombs!'

He went quiet then.

I was fair dinkum at the time, but my mates had no heart for that kind of thing.

My father did, though. By this time he knew I was comin' back to sleep in the dugout. He went down with a gallon of kero and burnt the whole place out. Denise watched him do it. All my clothes and everything I owned was burnt to ashes. All the dead bush around the yard caught fire too, so someone called the fire brigade who came and put it out. The firemen then told Dad to expect a bill from them since the fire was lit deliberate.

When I got home that night and seen what they had done, I went round to the front of the house and sang out 'You bastards!'

My father and his mates just laughed.

Then I yelled out 'You wait! Your turn is comin'. I'm going to burn the house down! Don't sleep too sound tonight, you bastards!'

They went real silent after that.

Before I left to go to a mate's place to sleep, I sang out 'Make the best of the time you have, arseholes!'

I went and slept at Robin Parnell's place. Someone must have told the coppers about all the ruckus. I knew Dad and his mates would be keepin' watch all the time in case I showed up to carry out my threat. I thought about burnin' the place down while they were at the pub, so they could see what it felt like havin' everything you owned destroyed, but then I worried about what would happen to Billy the Goat and the other animals that depended on me, so I forgot about it, sort of.

The police came around one night askin' for me. Denise told them I was out but she didn't know where I was. They told her to find me and get me to come home and have the matter out. They were sick and tired of gettin' reports and complaints from the other people in our street. They said for me to be there at 10.00am sharp, the next day.

When I got there, I waited for the cops to show up before I went in the yard. As usual, Dad and his mates were havin' a beverage on the verandah. One of the policemen said that they had completed their investigation about the fire and my threats to burn the place down. He said they were takin' the matter very serious because of the threat to life.

The other policeman was Flesser and he started on Dad and his mates. He said that they had been very violent towards me and had done the wrong thing when they had destroyed my dugout.

One seaman said that it was me that started the fire, it was just an accident that I had caused by havin' a little fire goin' all the time in the dugout, but I could see that didn't wash with the coppers. Flesser then asked if I had threatened to burn the place down. All the seamen said they hadn't heard me say nothin' like that. Dad said that that was a load of rubbish.

The copper said that he knew that I had threatened to burn the place down, but I was very lucky because the witness was not prepared to make a statement. He said that this street was becomin' a very dangerous place.

Everybody wanted the problem fixed and no more trouble.

Flesser then said that he had pretty much made up his mind to charge me with being a neglected child. He said that meant Westbrook, maybe till I was eighteen years old. That was a long time, he said. I was thirteen at the time.

Anyhow, after all the talk and palaver, the upshot was that I was to go and live at home again. In fact, I was to stay there as of that moment and Dad was to look after me and not treat me bad no more. Flesser said to me, 'Get home early every day and mind you don't get into no trouble.'

He gave Dad and his mates a good talkin' to about how they should be settin' an example. The policemen then stood up to go, shakin' hands and everyone friendly again.

Flesser called me aside and told me to let him know if Dad started bashin' me again. 'Come and see me and I will help you out, but no more trouble from you. Okay?'

Tears sprang to me eyes. Flesser said, 'Don't give them the pleasure of seein' you cry.' He patted me on the back and away they went.

Dad and his mates needed a drink. Denise went next door and rang for a taxi to take them to the Port Office Hotel. I went down the back-yard to give the animals some water and feed the dog.

The taxi arrived and as they were about to go, one of the seamen walked over to me and asked me if I had enough smokes. My Dad asked me could I clean the yard a bit while they were away?

I said okay.

His other mate gave me ten shillings to get myself some lunch and told me to be home early so there wouldn't be no more trouble. One of them laughed and said, 'Watch those coppers.'

I worked all day cleanin' up the yard. Robin Parnell came and helped me quite a bit. The men came home about five o'clock and were very pleased with all the work I had done, especially Dad.

From then on they did their thing and I did mine. No more fightin'. Dad even tried to be mates with me again, but I didn't want to. I just couldn't do it. It was hard on him and hard on me too, but at least it was peaceful at home again. He never bashed me again after that.

Later on in life I did forgive him. This was just before he died.

Anyhow, the Riverview Home plan was still on and it wasn't too long after all these events that a vacancy came up.

RIVERVIEW

Indeed, he [the Director of the Department of Health] attributed the large number of abscondings from Riverview to be in part due to the 'poor standard of accommodation and the physical conditions generally prevailing at the centre'.

The point was strongly made that, 'if a child in his own home was living in some of these conditions, then such may very well constitute evidence of physical neglect'.

Commission of Inquiry into Abuse of Children in Queensland Institutions
Leneen Forde AC, 1999.

The Salvation Army ran Riverview Home for Boys. My family meant to do the right thing by sendin' me there, but they had no idea what a terrible place it was.

They took me up by car, I can't remember whose it was, Dad didn't have one, might have been my uncle's. Anyway I remember there was a very long driveway leadin' from the road up to the buildings and the property went all the way down to the Bremer River.

There were very few children like myself whose parents were actually payin' for them to be there. It was just like the Lolly Farm, full of unwanted kids and the government was payin' the Salvation Army to keep them there. It was big business for them. They were bounty kids. All the churches cashed in on it. The more kids they got into their homes the more money they got. So kids were thrown into the homes from all over Queensland.

Riverview had a lot of very young boys as well as some older boys.

Plus there were live-in men who paid rent to be there. I soon found out that the men and the older boys were preyin' on the young boys. I don't know if all the staff knew about it, maybe, maybe not. I was a kid myself at the time.

To me this place was the pits. The food was horrible. It was actually rubbish. See, they used to go around to the restaurants and get the leftovers and make up meals from that. The very smell of the stuff they fed us made you sick. It was a miserable place this. No hope there.

I missed home, especially my dog and Billy the Goat. I missed my mates, especially Peter and Pancho.

About fifteen of us had to go to school. We went to the Dinmore State School. We walked to the Riverview station and caught the train from there. The headmaster was Mr Kennedy. We were all treated good by him and the teachers, but we were still 'Home' boys and sort of got looked down on. One kid said to me, 'You stink the same as your lunch.'

I was the dunce of the class, of course, but I didn't care. I hated school. All I wanted was to get away from there and be free. I used to think about tryin' to find the blackfellers from Bunyaville. If I could find them, I was sure they would take me in and look after me. I used to think about Banjie a lot. I got to kind of yearnin' for her.

They had line-up once a week in the Riverview Home. That was when Superintendent Smith would rant on and on about all the things we done wrong. Some kids used to get called up to get the strap. Some of them might have deserved it, but I don't really think any of them were bad. Most of them were just frightened and sad.

Bible-bashin' bastards they were in that place. Church was three times on Sunday. Boy, did I dread that day!

There wasn't much supervision in Riverview. Down at the piggery I was molested by one of the men who was payin' rent to be there. This was something new to me, and bloody disgustin' it was, and frightenin'! I reported this first incident to an officer. He just told me to go away, he didn't want to know. It took another fifty years, almost, before anyone would hear my story. I got to tell about it at the Forde Inquiry in 1999.

I drank some stuff that I thought was poison, I think it was kero, and

I did get very sick, but after a while I got better again. Then I ran away with another boy. We got on the train to Brisbane and went to Georges' Farm.

The Aboriginal family were gone without a trace. I heard later they were long gone even before I got sent to Riverview.

Me and the other boy got caught after about a week and were taken back to the home. It was a freezin' day and I remember waitin' on the verandah outside the office for someone to come and give me my beltin' for pissin' off. I was shakin' with the cold and fear.

Nobody thought to ask how come a boy reports being molested, then takes poison and then pisses off. Nobody cared. I got a beltin' for givin' them trouble, that was all.

Back to school and Headmaster Kennedy.

Him and the teacher had plans for the class dunce.

He bet me some money, I think it was a pound or something, in front of the whole class, that I couldn't get into the middle of the class with me grades. And then the teacher said, if I could get into the middle I'd get double the first amount of money. So in one term I went from the bottom of the class to about the third top!

I used to smoke in the boys' toilets at school.

Headmaster Kennedy knew I was smokin' down there so he calls me into his office. He says, 'If you must smoke, have a smoke in the office here,' and he give me the money to go over the road to buy a small packet of cigarettes.

When I get back he says, 'No more smoking outside of this office. I don't want the other children taking it up. I've got another packet of cigarettes in this drawer here, if you need it.'

Well I'm not sure whether he was callin' me bluff or not, but I did go and smoke in his office, quite regular. He would just walk out when I did it. But he kept his word and I kept mine. He was a good bloke.

Later in life, after I got out of Westbrook, he worked in a shop called Kennedy's Electrics, just down from the National Hotel in Brisbane. He would often give me money then. He helped me out on many occasions. He was very good to me.

Of course, when I did real well in class, him and the teacher expected great wonders from me, but I left not long after that and went back to Enoggera.

BACK WITH THE FAMILY

Children are committed to the care of the state for many complex reasons. History suggests that a major factor was related to parental incapacity to financially sustain the family unit.

Once information has been received, a departmental officer decides whether there are any identifiable child protection concerns. If it is determined that a child has been harmed, or is at risk of harm from a parent or other person living in the child's home, a child protection notification is recorded.

Commission of Inquiry into Abuse of Children in Queensland Institutions
Leneen Forde AC, 1999.

———————————

How I got back with my family was one weekend I was allowed to go home. It was just meant to be a little holiday, but I told my grandmother that I'd been molested at Riverview.

She was very distressed at this. For once, she didn't know what to do. She said, 'We can't do anything about this, we can't say anything. Who would think the Salvation Army would be running a brothel like this!' And she had to stop me father from going to Riverview to belt one of 'em.

Finally me father calmed down. He said, 'Yeah, we wouldn't survive runnin' the Salvation Army down with their great reputation during the war years.'

All this sexual abuse was eventually brought out in the Forde Inquiry in 1999, and I'll say this for the Salvos, they did pay me compensation when they found out about what was goin' on, then.

At least some of the churches have attempted to right the wrongs that were done in their name, in a small way. The main culprit at the time was the government, which was quite happy to let the churches be the scapegoats. Because the government was payin' the bounty for the kids to be in these places, they were the ringleaders in all this. I'd have to say the Beattie government and Anna Bligh did have the decency to open the Forde Inquiry. No other government would touch it! But the compensation paid to the victims was totally ridiculous, considerin' the sufferin' they endured for so long.

So I just didn't go back to the Home, Nanna and Dad kept me there in Enoggera. I would not have went back, anyway.

Over a period of time I came before the courts and was charged. But the Judge let me off because he didn't want me to go to Westbrook. I was charged with bein' a 'neglected child' and 'illegal use of a motor vehicle'.

The illegal use of a motor vehicle charge was made because me and me mate Joey, who was a bit older'n me, had found a Morris Kelpie in a car yard near where we lived. Now you could start these motor cars real easy, just by pushin' a button on the floor. Joey and me would take this car out of the yard every Saturday night. We wouldn't take it far, just around the block for a bit of a joyride. But this night we ran out of petrol and had to abandon it in the street. So we got caught.

So then things went on from one thing to another. My grandmother had to leave the place at Enoggera. She was on the verge of a nervous breakdown again.

Denise and me lived at home on our own for approximately nine months or it could even have been a year. I'm not sure see, my father had to go back to sea. To get money for food we had to sell some chooks, other people's of course, ours was long gone. Denise was twelve and I was thirteen and it was survival, just survival. We never let on to anybody that we was on our own or we'd be instantly shot into a Home. No one came around, people left us all alone.

The reason they left us alone was because Dad had invited a tribe of Aborigines into the house to look after us. This caused a lot of trouble in our neighbourhood because people were against the Aborigines, the whole street was against them.

Now these Aborigines were really good people. They looked after us, but they had a drinkin' problem and they'd often get a bit violent and the police would come to our place. Anyway, the Aboriginal people eventually left because the police was always comin' about their fights.

After one of the parties at our place, the police came round because there was a bad fight, blood and guts everywhere. Several police paddy wagons appeared and many of the Aboriginal people were put inside to be taken off to the lock-up. Anyway, I was off at me mate's place at the time and avoided bein' picked up, but Denise was also put into a paddy wagon and taken off to the Brisbane watch-house 'for questioning'.

Now Denise had about as much education as I had. She probably went to school for about three days of a year, if that. She was sat on a chair locked in a room by herself, and she stayed there for a whole day and a whole night. She didn't get anything to eat or drink and she couldn't even get out to go to the toilet. They were askin' her questions about me, about some information somebody had laid against me. Now as I said, night and day came and went and Denise is told to sign this piece of paper so she can go home to Mum. Denise could not read or write, but she signed that document and then suddenly there's a warrant out for my arrest.

My uncle and aunty took control of me through the courts. They became my guardians. Ken and Nell. They were related to me father.

Judge Andrews heard the case when it came to court and he put me in full custody to work as an apprentice jockey at Deagon, with a guy by the name of Murphy. And then if I left the job, I was to come and see him. I was on probation see. This judge more or less became like a guardian to me. Dormer Andrews was his name. He only had one arm, you know. He lost his other arm during the war when he was a fighter pilot. They used to call him the 'one-armed bandit' on account of it.

He was goin' to be the Governor of Queensland at one time and he was takin' a personal interest in my life to make sure I didn't end up in Westbrook.

Denise was put into a home. My mother couldn't look after my sister and she was put into a home. She was there for many years and her story's similar to mine. She broke out of all the homes, she was put into solitary confinement and probably did the same things I did. She's got her own story, her own book, which lays under her bed.

Anyway, I'm in Deagon, I'm workin' for the Murphys, there were two lots of Murphys and I seem to remember one of them had a horse named *Hortense*. Anyway these Murphys couldn't afford to pay me and after six weeks of practically no pay, I'd had enough. I says to the Boss one day, 'I'm goin'. I'm not workin' here no more, I'm goin'.'

He gave me all the silver he had in his pocket, so I goes to me aunty's place up at Newman Road, Wavell Heights.

She says 'What are you doin' back here?'

I says 'I've left the job.'

She says 'You've got to stay there and work that job. The judge said that. That's the conditions of you not going to Westbrook.'

And I said, 'The man wasn't payin' me, Aunty.'

She let it go. She said, 'Well you know you've got to go and see Andrews and see what he's going to do about this whole situation.'

So I did little jobs for her about the house and whatnot and this day come that we had to go into town and see Judge Andrews.

It was about four o'clock in the afternoon, in the District Court, I had to meet him in his chambers for him to sort out what the hell he was going to do. On the way there I was to pick up Bobby. Bobby was Ken and Nell's son. He had a disability. I had to pick him up in the Valley and bring him to the District court. Nell was workin' and she was goin' to come to the Court straight after work.

So on the way down to pick up Bobby, I pass Wunderlich's, which was a fibro factory, and I seen a big semi-trailer there. And I says to the driver, 'Where you goin' to mate?' And he says, 'I'm goin' to Melbourne.' And I says, 'Can I get a lift?'

I didn't plan this. The guy was just there. It just happened.

See, my aunty was always sayin' to me, 'I'm havin' you sent to Westbrook, I'm havin' you sent to Westbrook today. I'm not lookin' after ya... I'm havin' you sent to Westbrook.' So what was I to think? She always said later that she didn't mean it, but that afternoon, I thought, 'Oh shit, I'm goin' to Westbrook'.

There was no plan to this, I just hopped in the truck and went.

Apparently Andrews waited until seven o'clock that night. He said 'I don't want to sign these papers on him.'

And when I didn't turn up at all, (I've got his own papers in his own writin' here, somewhere) he said, 'I have no alternative but to sign him to Westbrook, because he didn't appear in this Court.'

It was quite funny about the semi-trailer driver, he must've been a good guy. I've got no clothes with me and I'm about seven stone in weight (45kg) and we get into Warwick and drive in the big service station there and a police car comes in. I get straight down on the floor of the cabin and he must have been thinkin' I'm a wanted criminal. No one was even lookin' for me at that stage. They hadn't even signed the papers yet and it had to go through the system, which takes time. But I wasn't to know that.

Anyway, he says, 'Oh don't worry about 'em.' He says, 'I know you're runnin' away from somethin' up there, but who's worried about that?'

He got me a meal, a hamburger or something of the sort, and I got to know him. He was a real nice bloke.

I told him about bein' a jockey and he says to me, 'You'd make a real fine jockey.' And he told me about these big stables that his relatives ran in Melbourne. And he said he'd take me to Melbourne and make sure they looked after me and I'd ride for 'em. But like a fool, I didn't go to Melbourne. I wanted to get to me friends that I knew in Sydney.

So anyway, I goes to Sydney. I lives in 24 Glebe Road, Glebe, with Grahame Cannon and Normie Gleeson and a lot of other blokes I knew who were much older than me from Grovely. They give me some money and blankets and that and I used to sleep out the back in a car. I was too young to get a job. Sometimes I used to sneak into the house and sleep on the floor, because it was freezin' in the car, but the landlady, Mrs Wright, was a pretty shrewd woman. She knew if anybody was sneaking into the rooms. She was runnin' a pretty straight boardin' house.

So I stayed at their place and they'd give me some money on Fridays. Terry Toon, he was in the army, he used to give me money too and buy me a meal during the week and that. And there was Jim Nichols. He done the same thing. So this went on for quite some time and I eventually ring me mother up. And me mother says 'Oh come home, come back to Brisbane, there's no problems, there's no problems at all.'

My mother wouldn't have known all about what had happened when I was livin' at my aunty's place, because there was very little communication between them two. She didn't know about Judge Andrew's conditions, so she really thought it'd be okay for me to come home. If she'd known, she would have told me to stay in Sydney.

In those days the police used to watch the airports all the time. There were always detectives there watchin' who was comin' in and who was goin' out. 'Course there was nothing like the volume of traffic they have today.

She sends down the fare and when I get off the plane in Brisbane, the coppers are waitin' for me. And from there I'm straight into the Brisbane watch-house.

WESTBROOK

Physical abuse

Corporal punishment was common in institutions, and was permitted under the Regulations in certain circumstances. The Inquiry found incidents of gross excesses in physical abuse in many institutions, beyond any acceptable boundary in any period. Aside from individual incidents of abuse, the Inquiry found in some institutions, at certain periods, a culture of physical punishment and brutality engendered or tolerated by the management. Westbrook, during the time when Roy Golledge was Superintendent, provided the most extreme example of such a culture.

Westbrook stood at the apex of the 'correctional' system for boys in care and was, without a doubt, its most feared institution. Sadly this fearsome reputation was only partially the result of its strict system for rehabilitating 'wayward' youths. The possibility of suffering some form of abuse at the institution was the greatest dread for the majority of boys in danger of being ordered to undergo a period of training there.

Commission of Inquiry into Abuse of Children in Queensland Institutions
Leneen Forde AC, 1999.

So I spend the night in the Brisbane watch-house with this other boy.

Everything felt damp and smelled of vomit.

He's sick. He's layin' down on this bunk they had in the cell. He actually went to sleep!

I didn't, or not for long.

Suddenly there is a crash at the door. I jump to me feet. I must have nodded off because for a moment I don't know where I am. The door opens and a copper comes in.

'Dinner,' he says. He looks at the other boy on the bunk. 'Get up,' he says.

The boy doesn't move.

'Get up and sit on the bed so's your mate can sit down and have his dinner.'

'He's crook,' I says.

The copper looks at the other boy. 'What's the matter with you? Do you need the doctor?'

The boy sits up and slowly shifts to the end of the bunk. 'No,' he says, 'I'm okay.' He sits starin' at the floor.

'Good,' says the copper. He points at me. 'You,' he says, 'you go and sit next to him.'

I start to say that I didn't want no dinner, but think better of it and go and sit down.

A Salvation Army man comes in and gives us each an enamel dish with some sort of stew in it. It looks like dog food. He goes back out and comes back with two spoons and two enamel mugs of tea.

'Eat your dinner,' says the copper. 'And don't make a mess.'

I suddenly realise how thirsty I am. I turn the cup so the handle is facin' away from me and gulp the tea down. The warmth of the tea spreads through me body, makin' me feel a bit better.

I finish the tea and start on the stew. It tastes as bad as it looks.

When the copper comes back to get the plates, I ask him if I could have a smoke.

'No smoking in here,' he says, but after a while a hand comes through the flap in the door. It has two cigarettes and a matchbox with one match in it.

The other boy sits up. 'Did he give us smokes?'

'Not us. Me. Get your own.'

The numbness has gone from my mind. 'How could I make two

matches from one? I'm thinkin'. Split it down the middle. Use your thumbnail. One smoke for now, one for later.'

As I draw the smoke into my lungs, my courage seems to flow back. I remember how black things had looked to me when I was in the lockup in Wauchope, the time I went down to Sydney on the back of Grahame Cannon's bike and then decided to hitch-hike back on me own. That had turned out all right in the end. Maybe Mum would put in a word for me, apply for custody or something. 'There has to be a way out of this mess.' Various ideas and schemes go through me mind.

I am feelin' so cold and miserable that I huddle in a corner and fall into a fitful sleep.

Breakfast was porridge and a cup of tea. And a smoke. They came and got us soon after.

Two coppers put handcuffs on us and took us downstairs to a car. They shut us in the back and threw our stuff, which was done up in paper bags, in the boot. I looked at the other boy. He was sittin' quietly with his head turned away from me, lookin' out the window at the brick wall.

We got goin' just as it began to get light. It was a foggy Brisbane winter's morning. There were just a few cars about on the streets but no pedestrians. They were takin' me to Westbrook and nobody knew or cared.

I started thinkin' about my animals. What had happened to Billy the goat and Tinker and Diddy? What was Nanna doing? In my mind's eye I could see her bustlin' about gettin' ready to catch the train for work. I wondered where she was livin' now. Maybe she was thinkin' of me, wonderin' what had become of me. If I could find out where she lived and get word to her, she would probably put in a good word for me. What about Mum? Would Aunty Nell tell her that I had been sentenced?

The coppers lit cigarettes.

'Can I have a smoke?'

'No.'

'I've got my own. In the boot.'

'You won't be smoking where you're going.'

'Well can't I have one now?'

'Shuddup.'

'Anyway, they won't keep me long.'

'You'll find out different.'

As the car made its way along the Ipswich Road, the sun came up and started to burn the morning fog away. It was going to be another clear, sunny, winter's day. I made a mental note of the landmarks and features along the way.

The road followed the railway line for most of the way as far as Riverview. I knew that part of the journey because by now I had been to and from Riverview by road and by train. From there we turned off onto the highway, which goes west, straight to Toowoomba. This country was new to me, mostly farmland and little scattered settlements. I made careful note, tryin' to remember everything I saw for future reference.

We passed through Gatton and started climbin' the range. The farm-land gave way to dense rainforest on both sides of the road. You could feel the air gettin' colder even in the smoky car.

Someone once told me that Toowoomba was Australia's biggest country town. It's at the top of the range, right on the edge of the escarpment. There are wide streets lined with trees, big houses on big blocks of land. There was fog about again and the streets looked dark and unfriendly. I couldn't see much.

Then we were through the town. The country now became flat and open, big bare paddocks with hardly any trees. And freezin' bloody cold.

Suddenly the car swung off the road and we were there. It was a bloody bleak place in the cold light, just these big wooden buildings on a bare hillside. My guts were churnin' with hunger and fear.

'Here you are boys, the Westbrook Holiday Farm. I'm sure you'll find your stay here most enjoyable.' Well, one of the coppers was enjoyin' himself.

'They won't be keepin' me here, long,' I told them again.

A short laugh and a grunt was all I got.

We were taken to an office and had our handcuffs removed. There were two men waitin' for us. The older one was very tall, a tough-lookin' bloke with a loud voice. He was obviously the boss. The other one was shorter and more thickset. I noticed that one of his thumbs was missin'.

'Good morning officers,' said the taller man. 'What wonderful specimens of Australian youth have you brought us today?'

There was a bit of chitchat while the coppers handed over our paper bags and got some papers signed.

'Did they give you any trouble on the way up?' The older man again.

'No, not really. That one reckoned he wouldn't be here long.' The copper jerked a thumb at me.

'Did he say that, did he?' He came towards me and bent down until his face was a few inches from mine. His breath stank of stale plonk. 'Mr Kolberg! Take that other lad to the store and give him his clothing issue.' He moved even closer to me. 'Reckon you're going to run, do you?' He was screamin' at me now. 'Well, we'll see about that, you humbug! We've got your measure, boy. Stand to attention when I'm talking to you, you waster!'

He went on and on like a lunatic. I thought I caught a bit of a look of sympathy on the policeman's face and I remember thinkin' I probably wouldn't cop a hidin' while they were there. But the next thing I knew I was pickin' meself up off the floor. My ears were ringin' and the side of me face was burnin'. He pushed me out of the door.

This was my first encounter with Superintendent Roy Golledge.

'Mr Kolberg!'

I was taken down to the veranda of a building where I could see Mr Kolberg and the other boy. He was naked. I was told to undress. I hesitated. Kolberg backhanded me across the other side of my face. He had a knob of bone where his thumb had been taken off and he really knew where to hit you with it. When he had finished knockin' me about, he shouted again, 'Get undressed!'

I took my clothes off and dropped them on the floor of the veranda where the other boy had dropped his. Kolberg went into a room and came back with some clothes. He threw them at us and said 'Put these on.' They were ordinary civilian clothes with numbers marked on them in Indian ink. He dropped some boots at our feet. That was it, all of our clothing issue. No underwear, no socks.

He pointed at me. 'Which one are you?'

'Fletcher.'

'Fletcher SIR!'

'Fletcher, Sir.'

He wrote the numbers on the palm of his hand and put an 'F' beside mine.

'Wait here,' he said and went back into the office.

After a while an older boy came up to us and said 'Youse are goin' to the orchard. Follow me.'

He took us to a paddock behind the building. Some other boys were there already. I was given a fork and told to dig. We weren't allowed to talk.

And that's how I spent my first day at 'the Brook'.

And a few more after that.

I got through my first few days at Westbrook because my mates Robin Parnell and Billy Campbell were already there. Everything about the place was lousy, but the fact that I had a couple of mates there gave me heart. Secondly, I got a letter from my mother sayin' that Andrews had told her that I would only be there for two or three months if I behaved myself.

'Three months isn't too bad', I thought. 'I'll cop it sweet and be a good boy.'

This was the daily routine. We got out of bed at 5.00am, kitchen boys earlier, and got dressed in the clothes we had folded up the night before and put on the floor at the foot of the bed. Then we folded our pyjamas, made the bed, marched to the row of taps, cold of course, which were in a long tin trough, washed our face and arms and cleaned our teeth if we had a toothbrush. When we had finished washin' we had to parade past the officer on duty and put our hands up like we were surrenderin' so he could see our palms and elbows, say 'Clean Sir', and fall into line to be marched to breakfast.

After breakfast there was muster. We had to stand under a roof on four posts in the yard. Sometimes there was a freezin' wind blowin', but we weren't allowed to go anywhere to shelter from it. We just had to wait there until Parade.

At 8.30am we had Parade and formed up into different parties. There was the Orchard Party, the Farm Party, the Dairy Party, and so on. The warders would yell out some announcement or other through a megaphone. Then we'd march off to our various jobs.

Our job in the orchard was diggin' with a fork. That's all we did. Just dig and turn the ground over. There were no trees. When you got to the end of a row you'd go up and start another one. No talkin'. You welcomed the sun or cursed it, accordin' to the weather. Most of the boys had chilblains and many of them had cold sores around their mouths.

Sundays were different, but I'll come to that later.

One day, not long after I'd arrived at the Brook, Robin told me that he was goin' to bolt.

They used to leave the side gate of the orchard unlocked. There was usually a screw or a sergeant hangin' round there, but not always.

At that time of year when we went for our morning wash, it was dark. Robin was goin' to wait for a real foggy morning and if there was nobody on the gate, he was goin' to get out that way. He asked me did I want to go with him, but I told him no. I reckoned I was goin' to be out of there in a little while, anyway.

His chance came quicker than I thought it would. He was just in front of me in the line for the taps and I saw him go. He was out of sight in a few seconds, but someone else saw him go and the hooters went off. They had truck horns mounted on posts around the place and they used to switch them on and off if somebody bolted, to get the chasers goin'. The chasers were boys recruited to go after any bolters. But it was so dark and foggy, I don't think anybody bothered chasin' Robin.

Later, when we're on Parade, this announcement comes over: 'Fletcher to the office.'

I went up onto the veranda and waited for Golledge to come and I was terrified. When he finally rolls up, he's as mad as a cut snake. He must've been talkin' to some of the boys, tryin' to get them to tell him something about Robin, but he wouldn't have got much out of them because I hadn't said anything to anybody and I was sure Robin hadn't, either.

Golledge accused me of knowin' about Robin's plan to escape.

I denied it.

He was rantin' and ravin', off his face. He kept repeatin', 'He's your mate. You must have known about it!'

I shook my head.

Finally he said, 'Take your pants down and bend over.'

The strap they used at the Brook was a terrifyin' thing. It was as long as your arm and a quarter of an inch thick. It was shaved down at the end so that it would curl around your hip. When they hit you with it, you got knocked forward. You couldn't help it. You were supposed to sing out 'Ooh Sir!' every time Golledge hit you. I didn't know that. If you didn't sing out, he just kept beltin' you.

I'd had some beltin's off my old man, but I never experienced anything like this. I kept gettin' knocked down onto the floor and Golledge kept tellin' me to get up and take it like a man.

He was puffin' and pantin' and shakin' when at last he had finished. He was totally out of control.

'I'll tell you something boy,' he said, 'when we catch him, and we will, you're going to get another flogging. I'll tear the bark off both of you, in public, in front of all the other boys!'

You've got no idea what a floggin' like that does to you, the damage it does to your mind. After that, I lost all interest in bein' a good boy. I made up my mind to get out of there, the first chance I got.

FLIGHTS FROM HELL

WARDER ASKS, WHY FLOG DECENT KIDS?
The warder, who has joined the chorus of complaints about the running of Westbrook Home said that, of the 130 boys at the home, about 90 were 'decent lads at heart'. 'Some of these kids are only 11 or 12,' he said. 'They are simply there because they are neglected children.'

The Toowoomba Chronicle
May 1961

A couple of weeks went by and there was still no sign of Robin. The terror of another floggin' began to fade a bit. I began to think that he might have shown them a clean pair of heels. I don't think it ever crossed my mind that he might have come to grief, died somewhere in the bush, or something.

To me now, getting away was everything. Once you were out and gone to New South Wales or some other state, nothing could happen to you. You'd have to be all right.

My bed in the dormitory was beside the desk where a warder sat all night. I couldn't do anything without him noticin', so it was impossible to sneak away then.

The kid in the bed next to me was called Charlie. Most of the other kids called him Schongie. He had been in Westbrook for a fair while. He was a quiet sort of bloke who kept to himself most of the time. He had run away from his aunty's place in Melbourne because somebody had been molestin' him there and he had made it all the way to Brisbane before he got caught and sent to the Brook as a neglected child. I used to talk to him a bit in our time off. He said he had a mother, but no father. One day I asked him why he didn't get in touch with his mother and ask her to come and get him. He said he didn't know where she lived. 'Anyway,' he said, 'I don't think she wants me.'

Schongie was the 'hose boy'. He had to move the sprinklers around the planted areas, so he knew the place pretty well. I tried to talk him into clearin' out with me, but he wouldn't be in it. He said he was definitely not goin' back to his aunty's place and he didn't have anywhere else to go. He was nearly seventeen and he knew they couldn't keep him there after he turned eighteen. All he had to do was stick it out for one more year and then he would be legally free.

Everyone liked Schongie, even the screws. He had a way about him that made people like to be around him. I asked him if he could come up with some way for me to get away. He really didn't want to get involved, but a couple of days later, he suggested to me that it might be a good idea to work it so that the screws took me out of the place.

'How the hell am I going to do that?' I asked.

'If you can get them to take you to hospital, you could get away from there. They wouldn't be watching as closely in hospital as they do here.'

'Holy smoke! What've you got to do to yourself to get to hospital?'

'Go mad. Let them take you away to get your head read.'

What a brilliant idea! Now all I had to do was find a way to do it. The whole place was a funny farm, so how mad did you have to get before they'd take you somewhere to see a shrink?

Schongie answered my thoughts. 'Attempt suicide.'

Schongie was also a 'shit ringer'. That was the name we gave to kids who had to empty the dunnies out of the warders' toilets. Shit ringers always stank and Schongie was no exception. They had to dig a hole in a part of a paddock called the 'shit block'. They had to put lids on the cans and take them down and empty them into the holes. After that they had to clean the cans and put them back. They couldn't help gettin' some crap on their clothes now and then. Our clothes were only washed once a week, so you can imagine what they were like by Saturday! Imagine what the shit ringers' clothes smelled like! They used to rotate most of the shit ringers, but for some reason, Schongie seemed to have the job permanent. Maybe it was because he was the hose boy.

Schongie used to go to a lot of trouble to keep himself clean. He asked me once if I thought he stank. I told him 'No, but your clothes sure do.' That seemed to hurt his feelings.

'Jeez mate,' I said, 'the whole place is on the nose, so don't worry about it.'

One of the rostered screws who watched us at night was called Bernoth. I didn't think he was a bad type, but a bloke called Ducie took a dislike to him. Something about not lettin' him go for a piss when he needed to. Ducie reckoned he was going to get him for that, so one night he smuggled an iron bar into the dormitory. It was part of one of those old gate hinges, with a knob on the end.

I woke up to the sound of bangin' and crashin' and saw Bernoth and Ducie sword fighting. Ducie had his iron bar and Bernoth had a poker from the fireplace. Ducie was definitely getting the better of the warden. He gave him a couple of beauties over the head before a sergeant raced up and grabbed him. Now these 'sergeants' were the toughest boys in the home who done the dirty work for the warders. But I know the sergeant saved Bernoth's life that night, because he couldn't have kept going much longer, the way he was bleedin' from the head.

Somebody had disabled the alarm by stickin' matches in the switch, but it wasn't long before Golledge was in the dormitory and Ducie was bashed down and handcuffed. They'd called the police and as they were taking him away, Ducie yells out 'I don't give a fuck what you do to me. I'm getting out of here, aren't I?' He was goin' to Boggo Road, see? (Boggo Road Gaol, Brisbane)

They took Bernoth away in an ambulance.

When all the excitement was over and we were told to go back to bed, Schongie said to me, 'Don't get to be like Ducie.' He seemed pretty upset by it all. I was too, especially seein' the blood spread all over the floor, the walls, and Schongie's and my beds.

There was a boy called John Litty who worked in the orchard with me and I told him I was thinkin' of makin' out I'm tryin' to kill myself by cuttin' me wrist. One day I made me move. I waited until I was well away from the warder, Hookie Woods, who was watchin' us, but not too far away from John Litty. I had a piece of broken glass with me and started hackin' into my wrist, I made sure there was plenty of blood runnin' down, I've still got the scar.

Anyway, John went runnin' off yellin' 'Mr Woods! Mr Woods! Fletcher's tryin' to kill himself!'

Hookey Woods came tearin' up and grabbed me. I gave my wrist a good deep gouge before he got the glass off me. I was pretty scared because I'd heard that you don't last long if you hit an artery.

He got me by the scruff of the neck and took me to the office. There was no matron or First Aid person at Westbrook in them days. Unless it was very serious, the staff did all the doctorin'. Golledge took a look at me and decided I wasn't going to die. They put some cow ointment on my wrist and bandaged it up. Then they sent me back to the Orchard.

My wrist was achin' like buggery. Fat lot of good that was, I thought to myself.

But about a week later, I got called to the office. Golledge told me that he knew it was just an act, but the Department wanted to have me sent for a psychiatric examination to cover themselves.

A screw called Essex was given the job of taking me to the rathouse to get my brains checked. We went in the Dodge ute, which was the one and only official vehicle at the Brook.

Essex took me to a place called Willowburn near Toowoomba. I couldn't believe my luck because that was where my grandfather lived. He had gone deaf and blind in his old age, but I would sure have liked to see him.

I talked to the psychiatrist for about two hours, at least. He even let me ring my mother and I pleaded with her to come and get me. She talked to the doctor, too.

The doctor finally told me that there was a lot more to declaring a person insane than just sayin' he was. I begged and pleaded for him to keep me at Willowburn, but he wouldn't change his mind. I asked him could I see my grandfather. He told me 'no'. 'Rules,' he said.

In the end he went and called Essex into the room and told him to take me back to Westbrook. Essex started making out like the long, lost father. 'You'll be all right,' he said, 'we'll look after you.'

When we got to the top of the stairs I jumped down them in one spring and took off. I reckon human beings can fly if they have to. My feet didn't seem to be touchin' the ground at all. Around the side of the building and over the back fence I went. There was a big open paddock there and I headed off across it as fast as I could go. There was a road around the outside of the paddock and I could see the Dodge tearin' along it. Whichever way I went, Essex'd drive to head me off. After a while a police car turned up. It stopped by the Dodge for a while and then both cars headed for a corner where there must have been a gate. I went like hell in the other direction and managed to get over the fences into another paddock before they could get back. There was a line of trees along a creek not far away and I headed for that. In there they could only chase me on foot. I kept runnin' and hidin' until I knew they had given up. It was pretty swampy in places and I got covered in mud.

Somewhere there was a railway goods yard, which I was tryin' to make my way to. I decided to keep goin' along the creek where there was cover. As I went along it, the bushes got thinner and thinner. It looked like they had been cleared all the way to the bank a bit further along, so I decided to backtrack a bit and wait until dark before goin' on.

I finished up hidin' in that creek all night, which was a mistake, because in the morning I could hear them comin' from all directions. There was nowhere to hide in the bushes so I climbed up a tree and tried to blend into the trunk as best I could.

It nearly worked. A couple of coppers walked right under the tree and would have kept goin' too except, just at that moment, a crow called out. They looked up and saw me and that was that.

I was caught.

The coppers were all right to me. One of them said, 'I expect you're hungry, son. Come down and we'll find you something to eat.'

I refused. I wasn't comin' down.

Essex then said that if I came down, I would be safe, nothing would happen to me, I wouldn't get no hidin', everything would be all right. He guaranteed all this in front of the coppers.

It was some hours before I did come down.

If I'd known then what was goin' to happen, I would have stayed up there, made them get the Fire Brigade and the television cameras and everything, but I was just a kid, silly enough to trust 'em.

By the way, that's how I got me nickname: Crow Fletcher.

Crowie.

You know, it's hard to describe your feelings when you're caught. It might have been worse for me because I had a lot of freedom before I got sent to Westbrook. I suppose you can compare humans with any other animal, say a possum or something. He may be sittin' in a tree and mean you no harm at all. He might even come right up close to you, once he gets used to you. But you catch him and try to hold him or put him in a cage, well then you'll have a different kind of animal altogether.

I was like a cornered rat. I had a pretty fair idea of what Golledge would do when I got back. Never mind the hunger and exhaustion from hidin' all night in that creek. Never mind the disappointment that my plan had failed and I had blown my chances for early release. The terrible, suffocatin' feeling of being caught blotted everything else out.

It wasn't long before I was back in the Dodge, handcuffed, with long-lost father Essex. The first thing he did when we got out of sight of the coppers was to backhand me across the nose. Every time I moved a bit, or even if I didn't, he'd backhand me. It was a long way back to Westbrook and by the time we got there, my nose and mouth were full of blood. I also had a big black eye.

Like I said, I was used to being bashed when my old man got pissed and in his moods. He had a lot of anger in him and he used to take it out on me. But there was no real hatred. Even Essex was just a thug without much feelin' one way or the other. He was pissed off because I'd made a fool of him and put him through a bit of trouble. Fair enough.

But Golledge hated me. He had hated me from day one. Maybe he would have killed me if he thought he could get away with it. Later in my life, when the Freedom of Information Act came in, I got hold of my files and the reports he wrote about me. He had no reason to hate me that much.

I've seen the hypocrite with tears runnin' down his face, sayin' he loved us all, that we were his boys, and a few minutes later, bashin' some kid to within an inch of his life for not singin' loud enough in church. He was a lunatic, a sadistic, plonk-drunk lunatic and a law unto himself at Westbrook. For a long while no-one was game to stand up to him. Admittedly they got rid of him out of Westbrook after the Schwarten Inquiry, but we had to go through hell to achieve that.

But I'm gettin' ahead of myself.

As you can imagine, I got another terrible floggin'. They took my hair off and put me on the Path.

The Path must have been Golledge's idea. It would be hard to think of anything more cruel.

It consisted of six parallel tracks, each twenty metres long and about two metres apart. There was a post at both ends of each track. You had to walk up and down between those posts all your spare time. You still had to do your day's work, but when the others knocked off, you went on the Path.

You had to keep walkin' quick. If you slowed down, they'd put a sergeant at each end to give you a smack in the head until you went quick enough for their likin'. If they went to the trouble of sendin' a couple of sergeants down, you got quite a few smacks, no matter how fast you went.

Can you imagine? You've had a floggin', your backside's black and blue, the sores are weepin' and stickin' to your strides, you've been up since five o'clock that morning and you've done a day's work in the paddock. You've had your hair off and there are chunks of flesh missin' from your head, torn out by the horse clippers they used. If the weather is cold, you've got a terrific headache. Your feet are blistered and bleedin' because your boots don't fit and you haven't got socks to wear.

And then you hear Golledge sing out: 'Mr Kolberg! Get a couple of sergeants down to the path and hurry that waster along a bit!'

That's what they did to Boots Hobson, not once, but time and time again. Can you wonder why he went the way he did? Boots was an innocent kid when he came to Westbrook, just a farm boy, and not real bright. They should have hung Golledge and his henchmen for what they did to Boots. And there are many men who must feel guilty about the bashings they gave Boots when they was boys at Westbrook.

Nobody was allowed to talk to you when you were doin' path punishment. You had your dinner standin' up, facin' against the wall. (Most probably you couldn't sit down, anyway, after the beltin' they give you.) When the other boys went into the Rec room after dinner, you stayed outside facin' the wall until it was time to go to bed. Some kids were even made to stand out at the foot of their bed for hours on end after the others had turned in. On Sundays they gave you a spell, only because this was visitors' day and they didn't want no witnesses to the path treatment. You had to stand under the shed, instead. If there was more than one of you, they made you stand in opposite corners. No talkin'. You never knew how long you'd be on the path. They'd just tell you one day, 'Okay, you're off the path.' Path punishment could turn some kids into psychopaths.

I did three months on the path that time. For half of that time I had my visits stopped through the State Children's Department. See Golledge didn't want my family to see the state I was in, the bruises, the scars on me back, the chunks of flesh out of me scalp. Bill Stokes had escaped some time before this and when they brought him back they put him in the Orchard. They gave him a pick and made him work on really hard ground so that his hands were made red raw. He was in a bad way from the floggings too. After thirty-seven stripes and scars all over his back, they stopped his visits until everything healed. They didn't want his people to see the condition he was in.

After I came off the path, I got into the Westbrook routine, or rather, I conformed to the routine and lived within myself. I thought of nothin' really, except escape. I couldn't even feel sorry for other boys when they got treated bad. Something inside me had hardened up.

They reckon you should learn to forgive, but sometimes it takes a big effort.

One morning Parade, Schongie's name was called. Havin' your name called on Parade usually meant only one thing, big trouble.

Schongie walked past us on the way to the office, tall and straight in his tar-and-shit-stained clothes and his big, awkward boots. I tried to catch his eye. He had a strange, self-conscious, almost embarrassed look on his face. He knew that every eye was on him but he didn't look at any of us. He seemed to be focusin' on some point in the distance. My eyes followed him until he disappeared behind the corner of the office. I suddenly got a feelin' that something was terribly wrong, but what was it? Did Golledge want to interrogate him over the bashing of Bernoth? Knowin' about something was a crime in Westbrook and Golledge used to belt confessions out of kids, like he had tried to with me. I felt a great surge of rage well up in me, but what could I do about it?

'Orchard party! Right turn. quick march!' Hookey Woods had the voice of a sergeant major. He carried a cane and used to tuck it under his arm like the army blokes do. I must've hung back a bit because he dug me in the ribs with it and told me to get a move on.

He was the orchard party chief, which was sort of like a foreman or leading hand. His job was to keep the boys workin', growin' the vegetables. Bernoth was back from hospital, but he wasn't too well. They must have taken him off night duty and put him in charge of the farm party. I spent nearly all my time in Westbrook in the orchard, which was the worst place of the lot, but it happened that one day they put me with the farm party. Must have been short of a man or something.

We were harrowin' the long paddock. It was a bastard of a job, walkin' up and down with this pair of draughthorses pullin' the harrow. We were takin' it in turns to drive the horses, but every so often we had to tip the harrow up to clear the grass and stuff from under it. There were five of us on the harrow crew. There was Mousey Morgan who came from Holland Park with Alan Fisher. They knew each other before they came to the Brook. Alan was the hardest boy in Westbrook. Big and solid, he could really fight. Golledge forced him to be a sergeant, so he was supposed to make sure that the boys in the farm party, us this day, didn't escape. He was very fit and a fast runner. Mousey in later years became known as 'Mad Dog Morgan'. Then there was Merv Reepsdorf, who was a nuggety little Murri, and a nice bloke, and Kenneth James McKeon who was a skinny, little, short-sighted boy, but pretty well-educated and very hated by Golledge. He was a good bloke too. And there was me.

Lunchtime came and went. Bernoth must have started feeling the heat and went and sat under a tree. I watched him. After a while he seemed to go to sleep.

'Here's our chance, Alan,' I said, 'I'm goin' to bolt.'

Alan and I had been plannin' something like this for weeks. I looked at Reepsdorf and McKeon. 'You blokes comin'?' They nodded but looked at Alan in shock. Alan Fisher only had about three more weeks to do at Westbrook. Why was he takin' such a chance?

'Okay,' he said. 'Best thing is to wait until Mousey gets right down to the bottom of the paddock and then walk down normally. If Bernoth wakes up, I'll tell him I've sent you down to clear the harrow. When you get over the fence, run like hell. I'm goin' to have to chase you and I sure as hell don't want to catch any of you.

There were some other boys diggin' up nut grass near where Bernoth was, but we didn't say anything to them. We just walked down slowly to Mousey and the horses.

'We're boltin'. You comin'?' we asked Mousey.

'My oath,' he said.

We were over the fence and gone. The paddock we were runnin' in had been ploughed and it was hard goin'. There was a line of trees in the distance which connected to bushland and from there we could get to the mountain, which was covered in bush. There were no roads there so the chasers would have to be on foot. It was late in the day and the light was fadin'. The important thing was to get to those trees before Alan caught up with us because Bernoth would be able to see everything from where he was.

As the first adrenalin-fuelled burst of energy began to give out on me, I realised that we still had a long way to go before we reached the cover of the trees. I also felt very thirsty and cursed myself for not havin' a drink from the water bag before we left. I hoped that there would be some water in the creek but knew that it would most likely be dry at this time of year.

Noticin' that the other boys were startin' to knock up too, I looked over my shoulder to see if anyone was after us yet.

Alan was already at the bottom of the paddock and I saw him hurdle the fence and come after us at terrific speed. At this rate he was goin' to catch up with us long before we got to the cover of the trees.

As he came up to us he shouted, 'Run, you bastards! You're slowin' down! Run! Run!'

We tried our best but he was soon beside us.

My lungs were achin' and my legs were startin' to go to jelly. 'I can't go no faster, Alan,' I said. 'Fall over and pretend you've hurt your ankle.'

'Like hell!' he said. 'I'm comin' too. Now run!'

I heard later that Bernoth was givin' a runnin' commentary from the top of the hill, 'Look at him go! He'll catch up with them no trouble at all. He's catching up with them! He's caught up! He's caught them. he's gone past them!' This caused a lot of hilarity at the Brook.

Alan went past us all right. He took on the leadership of the escape and ran ahead, urging us to run faster. Somehow that gave us heart and we struggled along behind him until we got to the trees.

He crashed straight through the creek, but we couldn't go on and dropped to the ground, gasping for breath.

'What's the matter with you blokes?' he said. 'Don't you want to get away? Come on, on your feet! We've got to keep going at least until we get into the scrub. We'll have a rest then.'

But he had to give us a couple of minutes to catch our breath. I went down to the creek and found a pool of water. It was brown and scummy but I drank from it like a camel and then splashed more water over myself, soakin' my shirt and shorts.

Alan kept talkin' to us, coaxin' us along and by the time it was gettin' dark, we were into the scrub and feelin' a whole lot safer.

We had got away all right and that gave us an indescribable feeling of elation. Westbrook was behind us and we were never goin' back. This time I had Alan and my other mates with me. I didn't have the fear and anxiety and loneliness I had felt when I had escaped alone. This time I would be right. We would get to Sydney and start a new life. I just knew it. The trick was to get over the NSW border 'cause then they wouldn't bring you back. You were right. That is, if you stayed out of Queensland until you turned eighteen. Well that was the law then. Later it changed.

Anyway, this was no time for daydreamin'. We reviewed our options and agreed that we would walk to Toowoomba that night and get down the range a bit where the bush was thick and the trains went slow. We would jump a goods train and lie down on top of a box carriage. The most dangerous part was gettin' out of the Roma Street goods yards when we got to Brisbane, but we knew the trains often stopped or slowed right down before then. When this happened, we would just jump off and scarper. We would stick together unless we got sprung, in which case it was every man for himself. We would then try to get in touch with Alan's mother to get some outside clothes and some money.

So we set off with Alan leading.

'I'm goin' to send Golledge a postcard from Sydney: having a wonderful time, wish you were here,' I said.

'Yair! Why don't you join us and we'll have some fun,' said Alan.

'Like we can use your head for a punchin' bag,' said Morgan.

'Bring Snifter. He can organise the athletics,' said McKeon.

'He can compete as well,' said Merv.

'But he'd better stay in front, 'cause we'll be right behind him,' said Morgan.

'Keep it down, boys. We have to get there yet,' said Alan.

'I'm goin' to get one of those wire recorders and send him a message, ¡Hey Sir, have a listen to this!¡ and the rest of it will be just laughin'. That'd kill 'im.'

'Keep it down, I said. They can hear you back at the Brook.' But Alan was laughin' too.

We went over the mountains and struck a road, which was pointin' in the right direction. This was much easier going and Alan upped the pace. We had to walk and run, walk and run, to keep up with him.

Around half-past nine we saw some lights in the distance.

'Must be Drayton,' said Alan. 'We'll sneak into town and see what we can see.'

'Good idea.'

We all had a raging thirst. None of us had any money, but at least there would be a water tank or a tap somewhere.

We slogged on till we got to the outskirts of the City of Drayton. They had all the streetlights switched on for us, all three of them.

We slipped into town like five shadows. Not a soul about anywhere, but the lights was still on in the pub. It must have been close to eleven o'clock by then. The law abidin' citizens of Drayton weren't abidin' strictly by the law as far as the drinkin' hours were concerned.

There it was. A Chevy ute parked outside the pub.

'You're the car thief, Mousey. Go and see what you can do with that ute,' said Alan.

We shrank into the shadows as Mousey crossed the road. He stopped briefly at the driver's door, then he got in and started the engine. The keys were in the ignition! The big Chevy leapt forward, kangaroo-hopped a couple of times, did an awkward U-turn and pulled up beside us in a great shower of pebbles and dust. Alan ripped open the door and he and McKeon piled in. Reepsdorf and I jumped into the back. Before we even had time to get a handhold, the wheels were spinnin', the ute was screamin' in first gear and we was off up the road.

Reepsdorf and I found ourselves jammed against the tailgate in a slimy, slithery mess. The back of the ute was full of meat! They had probably slaughtered a beast at the pub and this was the offal and the rubbish that the owner of the ute was takin' away.

We crawled and clawed our way to the front of the tray as the ute picked up speed and started swervin' into the bends in the road, throwin' us from side to side. I was absolutely terrified. I was tryin' to hold on, but everything I touched was greasy and slippery. Both of us were slidin' uncontrollably about all over the back. We were lucky not to have been thrown out. We banged on the roof of the cabin, yellin' for Morgan to slow down, but it was a long time before he finally stopped.

Alan stuck his head out of the window and said, 'What's the trouble?'

'We can't hang on in the back!'

'Get in the front, then.'

The door opened and Reepsdorf got in. I climbed in and sat on his lap. Almost immediately, Mousey dropped the clutch. We took off again with a terrific lurch. I always thought he was a lunatic, but this night he must've thought he was Stirling Moss. I'd never been so petrified in all my life. I kept pleadin' with him to slow down, but he took no notice at all.

'Alan, make him slow down,' I begged. 'Look at the fuel gauge. It's full. We can be across the border before morning if we don't draw attention to ourselves.'

Alan's face was dimly lit by the dashboard lights. He was smilin' and his eyes were bright. I've seen that same look a hundred times since on the faces of kids on fairground rides, total faith that nothin' can go wrong.

'Ah, stop squealin', Crowie. This sure beats walkin' don't it?'

In no time we were in Toowoomba and roarin' through the intersections at sixty miles an hour. Mousey didn't look right or left. Toowoomba was a pretty quiet place in those days, thankfully, so there wasn't any traffic about, but people would've heard us blocks away. How the coppers didn't get onto us, I'll never know, but there was no sign of them anywhere.

When you get to East Toowoomba, the road drops off sharply down the range. They've done a lot of work on that road since the 1960s, they've widened it and improved the surface and taken the worst of the corners out, but it still scares the hell out of me every time I go down it. The trip down the range that night was an absolute nightmare. The road was as rough as guts and the ute was just about airborne some of the time. But somehow, we made it to the bottom.

'Piece of piss,' said Alan and turned the radio on.

The road straightens out at the bottom of the range and Mousey seemed to be gettin' the hang of drivin' the ute, so some of my terror was startin' to fade. But suddenly the lights of a car came up behind us.

'Coppers!'

Mousey's foot was flat to the floor. We were roarin' along. But the lights of the other car were gainin' on us.

The next thing, the car pulls alongside us. There was a young bloke in it with a stupid grin on his face and he looks across at us and beeps his horn.

'He wants a race!' says Alan.

'Yer on!' yells Mousey. And just at that moment the hit song 'Apache' comes onto the radio.

For a while, we careered along side by side, but the other car began to pull away and it was soon in front of us. Terror set in again as Mousey tried to catch up and get round him. I looked at the speedo. The needle was flickin' just past 85, that's miles per hour. I don't know what it was in kilometres, but it's as fast as that Chevy would go.

Well, you can guess the outcome. There was a sweepin' curve in the road called Fruit Salad Bend where there was a big roadside fruit stall and that's where Mousey lost control.

As we left the road, the bangin' and rattlin' of the suspension went quiet for a second. Then all hell broke loose as we rolled over and over.

There was a terrific crash as we went through the wall of the fruit stall. We came to rest in a pile of fruit and splintered tables and boxes.

I must have been stunned for a few seconds because I have a vague recollection of being pushed about as the others jumped out, and then lyin' on the seat alone in the cab. The ute had rolled over and over and amazingly, ended up back on its wheels. The radio, though it'd been bumped off the station a bit and static was comin' through, was still playing 'Apache'.

Every time I hear that tune it brings back the memory of that night.

There was a strong smell of petrol.

I sat up and climbed out as quickly as I could. There was a street lamp nearby and I could see Mousey sittin' on the ground with his face in his hands. He had been thrown out when we rolled. Blood was oozin' through his fingers. I could hear Alan and Mac talkin' somewhere in the darkness. They were lookin' for Reepsdorf who had been thrown out too. They eventually found him by fallin' over him. He was groanin' and said he couldn't get up.

'We've got to get you out of here,' Alan was sayin'. 'There's petrol runnin' everywhere.'

They managed to pull him to his feet and started to drag him away. Reepsdorf was groanin' and sayin', 'Put me down, put me down.' But Alan grabbed him and tried piggy-backin' him. By this time he was screamin', so Alan laid him on the ground.

I pulled Mousey's hands away from his face. Half his nose was missin'. I helped him to his feet and he took off his shirt and held it to his face. Suddenly I felt real sick and dizzy and had to sit on the ground meself. I tried to vomit, but couldn't bring anything up.

After a while I became aware of another car with its headlights on. The driver was talkin' to Alan and Mac. These two had apparently stopped him by standin' on the road in front of him, flaggin' him down. He had been headin' west, back towards Toowoomba.

Alan opened the front passenger door. Mousey got in the front and they put Reepsdorf on the back seat. I heard Alan say 'Toowoomba Hospital' and then the car drove off.

The rest of us were shakin' and shiverin' but we knew we had to get away from there as quickly as possible. We started runnin' along the road in the direction of Brisbane, but soon decided that it would be better to stay in the paddocks because we were wastin' too much time hidin' every time a car passed by.

We walked and ran by turns for what seemed like three or four miles until Mac and I had had it and lay down in the grass to rest. Alan walked about restlessly, pleadin' for us to get up and keep goin', but I just went to sleep.

I woke up with Alan shakin' me.

'There's a farmhouse down there and there's a Holden in the shed. Mac's goin' to get it started. Come on, from here we're goin' in style!'

I got up and stumbled after him, feelin' like death. After a while, Mac appeared out of the darkness. 'The keys aren't in it. I'm goin' to have to hotwire it.'

We pushed the car out of the shed and Alan and I got in it. Mac ripped away at the wires behind the dash. It was pitch black so he was only going by feel. Anyway, he must have twisted the wrong wires together because the next thing I knew was that Alan has pulled me out of the car. There was smoke pourin' out from under the bonnet. McKeon had managed to set the car on fire.

So we just had to keep goin' on foot. We'd walk then run, then walk then run, until we couldn't run no further. My head felt as though it was goin' to explode. From time to time I could hear Alan's quiet voice warnin' me about some obstacle or other. 'Watch the ditch,' or 'fence here, Crowie. Mind the wire.' He must have helped Mac too, but I can't remember much about that. I remember drinkin' water from a ditch, which I was to discover later was half-raw sewage.

After a while we came to another farmhouse. We crept around it but couldn't find a car. There was a light on in the kitchen but it seemed that nobody was home. The back door was unlocked and Mac went inside and had a look around. He came back out and gave us a nod and we made a beeline for the fridge. There was a bottle of wine with only about a glass out of it and Alan pulled the cork and drank the rest down in one go. I found some Aspros and washed about six of them down with water from the kitchen tap. We ate everything there was to eat and then went into the bedroom and through the wardrobes. We got some clothes and a couple of pillowslips, which we filled with tins of food from the kitchen cupboards. The whole operation only took a few minutes and we didn't waste any time gettin' out of there.

We walked for miles and miles and miles, past Gatton, where we collapsed.

Before I fell asleep I took stock of the other two. Mac had that funny slit-eyed look that shortsighted people get when they're not wearin' their glasses. I watched him as he swept the sticks and pebbles away from where he wanted to lie down. He really was goin' by feel. He'd taken his glasses off in the dark, he must have had a hard time keepin' up last night.

Alan was bruised all over. The side of his face was swollen and one eye was nearly closed. He lay down carefully on his side, usin' his arm as a pillow and went straight to sleep.

I woke up tormented by ants. Mac had shifted and was sittin' under a tree. Alan was where he had slept, in the same position. The weepin' sore on the side of his face was covered in flies. Hell, what a mess!

We decided to hitch to Brisbane. The sun was well up and it was goin' to be another scorcher. We opened some of the tins we had stolen from the farmhouse and had breakfast. We cut a half-pound of butter into three pieces, dipped them in sugar, then wolfed them down. Then we went through the clothes. Alan and Mac got shirts that fitted them reasonably, but there was no shirt for me. It occurred to me to cut the number out of mine but I ended up just tyin' a cardigan round my neck and lettin' the sleeve hang down to cover it. Out of all the stuff we had stolen from the farmhouse there was only one thing left worth takin' with us, a packet of biscuits.

Breakfast over we got back on the road. We were all very sore, especially Alan, who was hobblin' along painfully like someone who had hurt his back. My head was clearer, but my body ached all over.

We didn't have to wait long for a lift. A semi pulled up. There was a lot of stuff in the front seat but there was room for me. Alan and Mac got into a sort of cage at the back of the cabin. The driver looked at me a bit queerly. He said, 'Been sleepin' rough, have youse?'

I told him that my Dad's car had broken down and we were goin' back to Brisbane to get some parts for it.

'Ah yair,' he said. 'What kind of car?'

'FJ'

'Ah yair. What's wrong with it?'

'Water pump, I think.'

'Ah yair.'

He had the radio on and I realised that there would have been something on the news about the wrecked fruit stall. I wondered what the cops must have thought when they first got there, all that dead meat everywhere. I went to try to turn the radio off, but the truckie said to leave it alone.

'It's a bit dicky,' he said.

After we got through Ipswich, a cop on a motorbike pulled us over.

The driver told me not to worry. 'It's only about the load,' he said.

But before the truck had come to a full stop I was out the door and runnin' as hard as I could go. I knew where we were. Riverview.

The boys were right behind me and I shouted to them to follow me. We went straight across the Salvation Army's paddock and down to the river. The bank at that spot was pretty overgrown and we struggled through vines and shrubbery to jump into the water. Then we half-swam, half-waded downstream.

After a while we crawled out of the water and lay down in the bushes. We were absolutely buggered. I remember tellin' Alan to get more out of sight, but can't remember much more until two cops turned up.

'It's no use trying to run, boys, you are surrounded,' said one of the cops. They were part of a combin' operation.

We automatically looked at the river and were about to jump in when the other cop said, 'The Water Police are on their way here now. Give up boys.'

There was no more go left in us, we had to give up.

The police took us to a farmhouse not far away from where they had parked their car. Through the scrub we could see all these other police cars, six or eight of them, and motorcycle cops, the bloody lot. The police were pretty good to us. They gave us cigarettes and didn't seem to be in a hurry to take us away, but they had to, ultimately, of course.

The bloke at the house was real good to us, too. He talked to us real kind and told the coppers, 'Don't take these boys away until I feed 'em.' He brought down sandwiches, cakes and drinks. It was like Christmas to us. He was a good man, whoever he was.

Then they handcuffed us and put us in the back of the police car. They took us back to Toowoomba under escort, there was a police motorcycle in the front of us and another police car behind us, and put us in the watch-house.

In the cell, Morgan was waitin' for us. His face was an absolute mess, black and blue and so swollen that I could hardly recognise him. They'd stitched up his nose at the hospital, but it was a pretty rough job.

'You blokes didn't last long,' he said.

He told us that Reepsdorf had been taken away before we got there. They had sent him to the watch-house from Toowoomba Hospital sayin' that there was nothin' wrong with him, but he had just lain on the floor, groanin'. They had to do something, so they got the doctor. The doctor told the coppers that he needed to go back to the hospital for X-rays and they took him away on a stretcher.

I didn't see Merv Reepsdorf again until I came across him years later in the Valley. He was walkin' usin' a frame. He told me that his pelvis had got broken in the accident. He was in hospital for about six months and when he got discharged he was free to go. He'd become of age and didn't have to go back to the Brook. But he was crippled for life.

In the morning, the coppers handcuffed us and took us to court, which was just next door. On the way over, I saw a bit of wire on the ground and picked it up. Those old-fashioned handcuffs were supposed to be easy to pick with a bit of wire, not that I had ever tried, but somebody had told me that. I thought I might have half a chance of boltin' from the courtroom.

We knew that we were entitled to three seven-day remands and were goin' to make sure we got all of them. Anything to put off goin' back to the Brook. We were charged with 'illegal use of a motor vehicle' and 'entering a premises with the intent to commit a crime'. The people who owned the house where we stole the stuff didn't want to press charges, so we got out of being charged with theft.

The hearing didn't take long, just time enough to read out the charges and grant the remand. During these proceedings, I worked the bit of wire around in the lock of the handcuffs. A bit broke off, so I bent it and started again, but the hearing was over before I could get the lock open.

Back at the watch-house, the coppers couldn't open the side of the cuffs I'd been fiddlin' with. They mucked around with their key in it for a long while then finally decided to take me to a workshop and get the lock drilled out. The handcuffs were made of hardened steel and it took quite some drillin' to spring the lock. They had to keep sharpenin' the drill. When they eventually got it open, the copper had a look inside and spotted the bit of wire. He made me empty my pockets and give him the other bit.

'The sergeant's going to be real happy with you,' he said.

When they got me back to the watch-house, they handcuffed me again and put me in a cell on me own. After a while the sergeant and two other coppers came in. The sergeant passed me a pillow off the bed.

'Hold this in front of you,' he said.

The other two coppers went and stood in the passage outside the door.

'This is for destruction of government property,' the sergeant said, and gave me a terrific thump in the guts. He hit the pillow, but it knocked the wind out of me and I went down.

'Get up sonny boy and get hold of that pillow.'

He kept hittin' me, either on the top of me arm, right on the point of the shoulder, or in the stomach until I couldn't get up again. Through it all I could hear a voice singin' out, 'Leave him alone, you bastards! Leave him alone!'

One of the coppers outside said, 'Shut your face you piece of shit or you'll be next!'

After the coppers went away and I got me breath back, I sang out and asked if there was anyone in the next cell.

A voice said, 'Is that you, Crow?'

I couldn't believe me ears. It was Schongie!

'Schongie! What're you doin' here?'

'Murder.'

'What?'

'I shot the farmer.'

'Was I dreamin'? There is always something unreal about a watch-house cell. The air has a closeness and a deadness which is hard to describe. All the normal background sounds don't quite reach there. And no matter how clean it seems to be, there is always an odour you'll never smell anywhere else. You can't explain it. Perhaps it's the smell of fear and despair, or perhaps it's just the blend of body odours of everyone who has ever been in there. The way you feel adds to the strangeness.

Schongie and I recognised each other's voices straight away but both of us needed a minute or so for the reality to register. I looked around the cell. Could this be a dream after all? My achin' body ruled that one out.

The flap in the door was closed but I went over and put my mouth against it. 'Schongie?'

'Yes.'

'What happened?'

'Weelu was a one-man town. It's a no-man town now, I shot the bastard.'

'Why?'

'He wanted to fuck me.' His voice was full of loathing. 'He was going to fuck me or send me back to Westbrook.' He went quiet and then I heard the sounds of him softly sobbin'.

'Jesus, Schongie, don't cry. You're makin' me cry.' But he couldn't stop and neither could I.

This was worse than anything I could have imagined. I leaned against the door and let the tears flow freely as I realised how much Schongie had come to mean to me. He was the boy in the home who gave everybody a lift, even the screws. He'd have a smile ready for you when you was feelin' like shit. He'd always say, 'One day this'll be all over, Crowie. Just try an' put up with it a bit longer'. He was an inspiration to everybody. He was not a violent person, he wouldn't hurt a fly. He always made people feel happy and anybody who knew him in Westbrook or in Boggo Road, would say the same thing, he was a good man. Me mate Bill Stokes will tell you that, you know, anybody. I had sometimes fantasised about getting out of Westbrook and meetin' up with him outside. I always felt that he had a steadiness and a strength that I could rely on when times got tough. We would get right out of Queensland, go south to Sydney, even to the west. We'd have a few adventures together, jobs, money, a life. That was my plan.

And now this.

I remembered his words to me, 'Don't get to be like Ducie, Crow.'

Schongie, of all people, a murderer!

The memory of that night in the Toowoomba watch-house is very clear in my mind, although much of it was dream-like. My body ached and I did eventually lie down on the cement floor and go to sleep, but I stayed at the door until Schongie had told me everything and had gone to lie down himself.

I did a bit of cryin' that night, for me and for him. It still hurts me to think back on it, but I'll tell the story as Schongie told it to me.

SHONGIE—Charles Leighton Schomberg

Some non-government institutions appeared to rely upon the labour of children in their care to supplement income. The organisations running these institutions profited from the labour of children through such commercial enterprises as farms or industrial laundries. The profits from such labour were not passed onto the children or their families...

Forgotten Australians
Senate Committee Report on Australians who experienced institutional
or out-of-home care as children. 2004

They had a system at the Brook where they would take boys out of the home and licence them out as farmhands. The boys were supposed to get paid for their work, but I don't think anybody ever saw those wages. They'd look out for the boys who wouldn't give no trouble and use 'em as slave labour.

That day, when Schongie was called up on parade, was the day they told him he was goin' to go to work for a cockie on a farm at Weelu, a tiny place a few miles from Goombungee on the Darling Downs.

It was late afternoon when Schongie and the farmer arrived at the farm and the cows were due for milkin'. A room had been prepared for Schongie, which was pretty unusual. Most Westbrook boys who went to work on the farms had to sleep in an outhouse with the animals.

Schongie had never done any milkin' before but he got the hang of it pretty quickly and worked with the farmer until all the cows were done. It was late August and the season was beginnin' to turn, but it was still pretty cold after sundown. The farmer was dairyin' for cream and the milk had to be separated. Normally the farmer's wife did the separatin', accordin' to the farmer, but she had something wrong with her and was goin' into hospital. The milk from the morning's milkin' was still in the dairy so the separatin' of the cream from the skim milk had to be done that night.

It was all new to Schongie but he got stuck into it after tea so that by midnight everything was ready for the next day, when the farmer said he would tell the boy about all his other chores.

The farmer woke him before dawn.

'We'll bring the cows in and yard them. I'm taking the missus to Toowoomba after breakfast. You can start milking then. When you've finished that, you can do the separating. There's some chaff wants chopping, but I'll probably be back before then.'

Schongie soon got into the routine of dairy farmin', which was really just one endless chore like movin' the hoses at Westbrook. He and the farmer got up in the dark and after a cup of tea went out into the freezin' darkness to bring the cows into the bails. He didn't mind the work, he was used to gettin' up early and workin' long hours for a wage he never saw. He didn't even mind the loneliness of the isolated farm. Like most Westbrook boys, he was a solitary person by nature. Anything was better than Westbrook, even workin' seven days a week from morning till night on a government-backed slave-labour scheme. Not all farmers were guilty of this treatment of the boys who were sent to them, mind, but many of them were. See, they picked the boys from the homes who would be good as slaves for this kind of thing.

As the weeks passed, the farmer found that he needed to do more and more business in town, so Schongie finishes up doin' most of the separatin' himself, and many of the other chores as well. The farmer woke him early, had a cup of tea with him and then went back to bed, for all Schongie knew. While he was happy to be left alone with the work, Schongie resented the farmer's complaints. He didn't have a good word to say about anything and he had to listen to the farmer run him down as a lazy so-and-so at the tea and biscuits sessions after church.

After some weeks it became pretty clear that the farmer's wife was not comin' back. Schongie had not even seen her, himself.

He asked about her once or twice, but the farmer didn't want to talk about her.

Their meal breaks were mostly taken in silence, then after dinner there was the radio before bedtime. Schongie noticed that this was when the farmer was most likely to talk, and the subject was always sex.

Schongie didn't like talkin' about sex. He'd got out of Melbourne because of it and had seen some really disgusting things at the Brook, so naturally he got scared. There was nowhere for him to go after dark except his room and he used to go there and close the door before the news on the radio was finished.

If the farmer came in and wanted to talk, Schongie pretended to be asleep.

One Sunday the farmer went off to play tennis somewhere, leaving Schongie alone on the farm with instructions to do various jobs after he had finished the separatin'. When he came back, late in the afternoon, it was with the usual complaint: 'What have you been doing all day?'

'I've done the cream and cleaned the separator; I've washed out the dairy and chopped enough feed for tomorrow. What more do you want?'

'The milking shed's a mess and I told you to wire up the top gate. You haven't done that, have you? If the cows get out of that paddock, we'll be chasing them for miles. You'll have to do that tomorrow, now. Bring the cows up and yard them. We'll do the milking after church.'

Schongie turned on his heel and walked off without sayin' a word. He hesitated a moment by the shed, then went in and got a length of wire and the fencing pliers. He was back half an hour later with the cows. He yarded them and closed the gate, then put the pliers back in the shed.

When he went into the house, the farmer was sitting at the kitchen table with a cup of tea and an open packet of biscuits in front of him.

'Fix the gate, did yer?'

'Yes.'

'Good lad. Make yourself a cuppa and then go and have a wash and get dressed. We're going to have to get a move on.'

Schongie made his tea and sat down at the table. The farmer's mood had changed and he was suddenly very talkative. Schongie looked down into his cup.

'There's a new girl at tennis, now. She's a real looker. None of the blokes could take their eyes off her. I might take you along to the tennis one day and let you have a look for yourself. She'd be about your age, just about ripe for the picking.'

Schongie jumped to his feet.

'I don't like that kind of talk.' He began to stutter, 'Y-y-you shouldn't talk that way about people!'

'Arr, come on. You're not tryin' to tell me you wouldn't enjoy a bit of hanky-panky if you got the chance!'

Schongie brushed past the farmer and went to his room and shut the door. He sat on the bed and tried to pull himself together. 'Just stick it out for a few more months, just few more months and you'll be free', he told himself. 'You'll have money and you'll be able to go anywhere you like, even have a holiday! Just stick it out. Just stick it out.'

The bedroom door opened. Schongie could see the farmer standin' in the doorway. Then he took a step into the room.

'Look sonny, you don't have to upset yourself just because I said something about a piece of fluff. There's no harm in talking, and looking's free, as they say. I can't see what you're so upset about.' He paused and moved closer to Schongie. 'Unless you don't like girls. ' He had a nasty grin on his face and took another step closer. 'Yair, maybe that's it, maybe that's the problem. Maybe you prefer it the other way. I've heard what you Westbrook boys get up to when the lights go out.'

He suddenly pounced on Schongie and tried to wrestle him to the bed.

Schongie pushed him off, knockin' him to the floor. 'Get out! Get out!' he screamed. 'Keep away from me! Don't touch me!'

The farmer got to his feet. His face was white and his voice was shaky and hoarse. 'Okay sonny, if that's the way you want to play it, you're not coming with me this afternoon, you can stop here.' His whole body began to shake then. 'And tomorrow,' he hissed, 'tomorrow morning, I'm taking you back to Westbrook!' He turned and walked unsteadily down the hall.

Schongie was terrified. What would the farmer do now? Would he come back into his room after he'd fallen asleep? Try again? He'd better get the hell out of here. But where could he go? There was nowhere to run to, nobody to run to.

Then he remembered the rifle the farmer kept in the house, in a corner just outside the bathroom. Schongie didn't like violence, it made him sick, but he grabbed the rifle.

He heard the farmer comin' out of his room, so he ducked across the hall into the kitchen and cowered against the wall behind the fridge. The farmer couldn't have seen him because he walked straight past the kitchen into the bathroom. Then there were splashin' noises coming from there.

When he was cleanin' his teeth at the hand basin, the farmer was mutterin' something but didn't turn around. Schongie pointed the rifle at the back of his head and pulled the trigger.

The farmer crashed to the floor. Great globs of blood oozed from the back of his head. He face twitched for a while and his arms spasmed, but he was soon still.

Schongie was in shock. He stood over the body of the farmer until all movement had stopped. Then he put the rifle back in its place beside the bathroom door and went into the kitchen and sat down. His cup of tea, now cold, was still on the table. He gulped it down then automatically put the kettle on again.

In a daze, he walked around the rooms of the house. He even went into the farmer's bedroom, he had never done that before. There was a rumpled double bed and an open wardrobe in it. Clothes were scattered about. The wardrobe door had a mirror on it. Schongie told me he went up to it and stared at his own reflection. He couldn't believe what he was seein'. It was years since he had last looked into a mirror and seen himself. There's no mirrors at Westbrook. He'd been just a little kid when he last saw his reflection. Starin' back at him now was a tall young man, tanned and wiry. Strong lookin'. Who the hell was this?

The sun was settin' and the house felt gloomy and strange. He went back to the kitchen and made himself another cup of tea. He wolfed down the biscuits on the table and sipped the tea. Why was everything so quiet? Where was the farmer?

When it was quite dark, he switched on the lights and looked around the house again. The last room he looked in was the bathroom.

The farmer lay where he had fallen, his legs buckled under him and his body thrown back. His eyes were open and his lips were slightly parted, as if he was about to say somethin'. Schongie also noticed that the dirty bastard had wet himself.

He pushed and twisted the body to free the legs, then took hold of the ankles and dragged it to the back landin' and down the stairs. He could feel the head bouncin' on every step.

There was a tankstand beside the house, which had been enclosed with corrugated iron. He dragged the farmer in there. It was pitch black in that little room. Once inside, he carefully stepped over the body and went outside, closin' the tin door behind him. A storm had been brewin' and the first cold gusts of wind were sweepin' across the farm. He went upstairs into the house.

Schongie said in the cells that day that he had just snapped. Something made him snap. He thought about it a lot, goin' over and over in his mind about it. He said it wasn't even the fact that the farmer had tried to rape him that made him act that way, it was the threat of goin' back to Westbrook.

I reckon it was Westbrook that killed that farmer, not Schongie.

We was walkin' time bombs.

Well, still in a daze Schongie washed the blood off himself and then he got some biscuits and some of the farmer's clothes and what money was kept around the place. Then he walked towards Toowoomba.

He dumped the food for some unknown reason, he was still in shock, I suppose, and walked all the way to Toowoomba. He made his way down to Sydney and while he was in Sydney, took his clothes to the dry cleaners to get rid of the bloodstains. He then went to Melbourne, to the home of one of his relatives. This person told him to give himself up to Homicide, which he did.

The police held him there till someone came down from Queensland, Glen Patrick Hallorhan, and they charged him then with murder. They took him back to Sydney and went to the dry cleaners shop, verifyin' that the dry cleaner was there and askin' him about the blood and whatnot. They took him back to Brisbane, then back to Toowoomba and from the Toowoomba watch-house to Goombungee.

He showed them exactly what he had done and told them the story about the farmer tryin' to sexually abuse him. Then he was taken back to the Toowoomba watch-house at the time Alan Fisher and all of us was there.

Schomberg was sentenced to life in prison at Boggo Road gaol. The story on the road is that the politicians' influence in the gaol got Schomberg to say that none of the other stuff ever happened, that he just shot the guy in cold blood. So, after much pressure was brought to bear on him, Schomberg did come out and say that he'd made up the bit about the farmer jumpin' on him. Schomberg did make this statement. It was later read out in Parliament House, apparently for the farmer's mother or wife, I'm not sure of which one it was, one of 'em, to clear the farmer's name for them.

They pushed him into saying this thing by tellin' him life would be a lot easier for him in gaol if he came out and said it, so he said it, much, much later. But he told me the story I've just told you about what happened that night many times.

He spent many years in gaol. He was put in the criminally insane ward at Wacol where they injected him with all sorts of things and put him in this tiny little cell, a sad place Wacol, and then he got out of there and was put back in the prison system. He was released and nobody seems to know the date, the time or anythink, and naturally, being a murderer, he's supposed to be on parole for life.

Whatever happened to Schomberg then, nobody knows, but for a long time I sent him letters and he sent me letters and this went on for many years. I always kept in touch. And then everything went quiet. That would probably have been the time they put him in the criminally insane ward and give him many little pills to help his brain become dead. That's about all we can say about Schongie.

There [I]is[I] just one other thing. When the jury came back to the judge at his trial, they recommended strong mercy for this boy. They sure gave him mercy. He done twenty-six years. They forgot about him, lost him in the system.

Where he is today? I don't know. Whether he's dead or alive, I don't know. No one seems to know. Don Cameron remembers a time when he was in Boggo Road and Schongie was there and he said that he couldn't take no more and was goin' to commit suicide. It certainly wasn't the Schongie that we used to know in Westbrook talkin'. Somebody else. What they'd turned him into.

Yeah, because you see, as I said before, it was the Brook that really killed the farmer. It was the thought of goin' back there that made Schongie snap. Westbrook is responsible for a lot of bad things that happened. Which brings me to Boots Hobson.

BOOTS HOBSON

Apart from the floggings or beatings described by the witnesses, a number also referred to the practice of certain boys being appointed as 'sergeants'. Their role appears to have been to assist in the maintenance of discipline among the other boys.

One witness, appointed as a sergeant against his wishes, stated that his experience of being a sergeant has rendered him devoid of humanity and destroyed him spiritually. He appeared to have suffered great emotional trauma from being forced to brutalise other inmates.

Commission of Inquiry into Abuse of Children in Queensland Institutions
Leneen Forde AC, 1999.

———————————

Boots Hobson had very big feet and they had to make special shoes for him and all the boys would chuck off at poor old Boots. He probably had a thing in his brain about havin' these big feet.

Down in the orchard where he used to work, one of the boys, a sergeant, was bashin' him and makin' him run up and down the path with a pick axe to weight him down. The officer in charge there, called Seymour, didn't care. They thought it was quite funny. As he'd get to one end they'd knock him down and then as he'd get to the other end, they'd knock him down again. This went on for quite some time. I was in between this, workin' on one of the beds of vegetables with a bloke called Liddy.

Boots fell right down beside me and he said, 'I'm going to kill that fuckin' bastard, I'm going to put the pick through his fuckin' head.'

And I jumped up and ran up to the sergeant, and it was a very, very dangerous situation 'cause I could have got smashed to bits meself, and I said, 'Don't touch him no more, don't touch him no more. He's gunna kill ya, don't touch him!'

Seymour sang out and said 'No more of that, now, no more.'

I do believe that if there was no intervention at that time, because he proved later how violent he could be with all those people he killed, he was gunna put the pick straight through that sergeant's head. He couldn't take no more.

Anyway, to cut a long story short, he had many hidin's off the sergeants and was bashed a lot in the place. Golledge give him plenty of beltin's. Anyhow when he left Westbrook he got a job on a farm, I think it was around the bottom of the Range in that area, the Toowoomba Range.

I don't know what led up to this, but he shot the farmer and the farmer's wife and the pigs and the birds. He just went berserk. And he was sent to gaol, naturally, for life. And in gaol he killed the officer in the Number 2 Division in Boggo Road, where they put me as a child because I gave 'em up in the Schwarten Inquiry, but I'm gettin' ahead of meself here. He put an iron bar through the officer's head. Boots killed him, apparently because he was chuckin' off at him about his feet. They drugged him up and they put him in the criminally insane ward and they kept him there for many, many years.

They brought him back to Boggo Road gaol and he died on the oval at the gaol from a massive heart attack. And that was the end of Boots Hobson. He was only about thirty at the time.

BACK THROUGH THE GATES OF HELL

To the inmate, Westbrook must have appeared a punitive establishment in which he was required to sit out a period of detention, the length of which he did not know, except that it could continue until he attained his 18th birthday. To those detained for any considerable length of time it must have meant stagnation and mental anaemia, a condition conducive to the breakdown in morale and discipline and fruitful ground for the incorrigible to work upon...

Westbrook Farm Home for Boys Inquiry,
Schwarten AE 1961, Queensland Government

Back to the watch-house at Toowoomba.

We were taken to the Magistrate's Court. Kearney, a very much-feared Magistrate, was waitin' for us. We were charged with 'illegal use of a motor vehicle'.

'Alan Edward Fisher, Alfred Donald Fletcher, Kenneth James McKeon and Dennis Morgan, I remand you to the District Court for these charges to be heard against you. Have you anything to say?'

'No Sir.'

'Okay. Now you've had three seven-day remands in the Toowoomba watch-house, you get no more. And I'll tell you what now, go back to Westbrook and tell all those boys at Westbrook that if anyone comes before me for any charge whatsoever, I shall give them two years straight on their sentence. Got that?'

'Yes Sir.'

'Righto.' He nodded to the coppers.

The police then took us back into the Toowoomba watch-house where they done the paperwork. Then they came into our cells.

'Up boys, the picnic's over.'

They handcuffed us up, with about six police, two on each side of us, and they started to take us out. As we went past Schongie's cell, I gave a little kick on the door and said 'See ya Schongie,'

Schongie said, 'Oh, I feel sorry for you, Crow, but it'll all pass, mate. One day we'll all be out of here. '

I said, 'Yes, Schongie.'

Poor Schomberg didn't know that he wouldn't be out until about twenty-six years later, none of us knew that, then.

So out we went. The watch-house keeper was ringin' Golledge up sayin' 'They're on their way.' And you could hear Golledge saying through the speaker, 'And we are waitin' for them.'

Okay, into the police car and on our way back to Westbrook.

It was a silent trip back. We knew what we were gunna get. we knew what sort of floggin' this was goin' to be. Well, we entered the gates of Westbrook, we entered the gates of hell. And I believed in hell after this punishment.

About a hundred and twenty boys are all in a straight line out the front of the office as we arrive. The police empty us out and standin' there are Kolberg, Golledge, Essex and some other officers.

Golledge stands in the front door screamin' 'Youse are finally back are youse smarties?'

No one said a word, just looked. The police handed over the papers, they said goodbye, jumped in their car and off they went.

Golledge says 'Take 'em down to the Big Rec. We'll make a public floggin' of this lot, in front of everybody.'

Kolberg went up very quietly and said, 'Mr Golledge, that Fisher's a pretty tough man and if these boys turn on us they'll start a big riot down there and goodness knows what might happen.'

Golledge says, 'Well, okay. We'll flog 'em in the office, but keep them boys outside so they can hear the screams and we'll terrify them so they'll know not to run.'

Okay, we're in the office and Golledge he starts screamin' out: 'Why lads? Why did you do this to me? And you, Alan Fisher, you're the most trusted boy in this home. I'll never trust another boy again, after you, Alan. I don't want to do this to you boys. I don't want to belt youse, I love youse all. To do this to us, to do this to this Home. You've taken a car, you've rolled it over, you've got Reepsdorf in a critical condition in the hospital. Lads, I've no alternative. '

Then next minute he lunges at McKeon and grabs him.

Poor Macca. I was behind Fisher. I got behind Alan quite deliberate, because I knew that Golledge's arm would eventually give out. I knew it'd be better gettin' a floggin' off Kolberg, than getting' a floggin' off this lunatic.

'Down with ya pants lad. Get the pants right down and pull that shirt up.'

Then he started. And he kept goin' with this big, long belt. It was a big, thick belt about a quarter of an inch wide, taperin' off at the end so it could really bash into ya, it came off a horse dray this belt, about three feet long and wrapped around his hand. And he's into McKeon. One, two, bashin' into him. You could hear the crackin', and this went on and on and on.

McKeon's gettin' up off the ground. 'No more, Sir, no more, Sir. ' And Golledge says 'I'll give you this McKeon' and he just kept goin'.

I've never seen a floggin' like it. I would say he got at least thirty to forty stripes. The blood by this time was startin' to run down McKeon's back, down his backside. You could see the welts comin' out and the marks all over his body. It made you sick.

McKeon's worn out by now. He's collapsed on the ground; he could take no more. And Golledge realises the McKeon's about to faint or pass out, plus, Golledge's shoulder's givin' out on him.

Then he grabs Morgan and he's half-way through Morgan, givin' him a tremendous floggin' and he says 'Mr Kolberg, you'll have to take over, me shoulder's gorn again. These parasites, these humbugs, we've got to teach them a lesson.'

So Kolberg takes over. He never give you as many of the belt as Golledge did, but when he give you the belt, each strike was equal to three strikes of Golledge. He brought it down and somehow he could flick it. Each time he brought it down, a nice little chunk of your backside disappeared.

So Morgan's screamin' and he hits the deck, you know, up and down, up and down.

Golledge goes and opens the door, the door was shut, and he yells, 'I hope you lads out there hear this. Youse will all be next, if any of youse are runners!'

Then it was Fisher's turn and strong as he was, he copped it and he had to sing out, 'Ooh Sir! Ooh Sir! Ooh Sir! Ooh Sir! Ooh Sir!' This went on for a long time. And then it was my turn.

I had hid behind Fisher, hopin' that they'd be tired by the time they got to me, I'd be last to get a floggin', when they was tired. But oh, to watch all them belted the way they were, I felt sick to me stomach, my head was spinnin', 'Oh, if only I could get out of this place was all I was thinkin''. I was ill.

Then he grabbed me. And into me, what a humbug I was and a no-gooder and a waster and all this. Golledge was singin' out, 'You waster, Fletcher. You are nothing but a waster! I'll break you, lad, I'm goin' to break you. You're going to be here for many more years and I will break you, I will smash you!'

So into me he goes, Kolberg, 'One, two, three. '

I'm fallin' down to the ground. 'No more, Sir! No more! Ooh Sir! Ooh Sir!' This time I could feel me arse splittin'. Chunks of flesh were lifted off me...

Anyhow, somehow it's all over and I don't know how. We were on our feet, and we could feel the blood runnin' down the backs of our legs.

'Get the horse clippers, Mr Essex, get the horse clippers and off with their hair!'

So into us with the horse clippers, it only took about five minutes to do the lot of us, they're them clippers that they cut the sheep with. Anyhow a big chunk they took out of my head and Morgan had chunks out of his head and McKeon. McKeon's glasses were smashed on the ground. They walked over McKeon's glasses, so poor old Macca now can't see. He's got no glasses! Anyhow they ripped all our hair off, then Golledge went out the front and he said, 'Down to the path. I want 'em walkin' up and down that path. All day, today.' So that whole day, bar the meal breaks, we marched up and down, up and down, up and down. No talkin', marchin'.

They took us down to the shower block before the other boys had their shower in the afternoon and naturally, they give us a cold shower and one of them said they should throw salt over our wounds. They were lookin' at each other and lookin' at our backsides and our backs. They had all turned purple and red. You could see the congealed blood on each one of us, it was really a sight to see, this. It was something like what you'd see in an old movie of what they did to the convicts, it was the same sort of treatment, it was no different, or a prisoner of war camp.

Anyway, back out, and marchin' up and down again after our shower, until the other boys have had all their showers. We had to stand up when we had our meals, and this was the routine, day in, day out, not stoppin'. At night time when we laid in bed, we had to lay on our stomachs because the pyjamas would stick to the blood and ooze on yer back and yer bum. Well, you couldn't lay on your back anyway because it was too raw, too sore. We slept on our stomachs for many weeks, it was a long time, and the awful thing about it was, when you got up in the morning, your pyjama pants would be stuck to your back and your bum! You had to peel them off and you know, the pain was excruciatin'. And so the scabs never got a chance to heal. You had your wounds a long time because we had no dressin's. They wouldn't give us no cow ointment or anything to help us. We just had to put up with that. And how long it took for that to heal. You couldn't sit down properly, with the pain.

Anyhow, we all had to go back to Court some two or three months later, I'm not sure of the date, and we went before Judge Andrews. And Andrews said to me 'You know Fletcher, you could have been out of here. I was making it my personal business to get you out of here within three months.'

And I said, 'Sir, it is not my fault. These people, what they are doin' in Westbrook. They're beltin' us and floggin' us and I had no alternative but to try to run away.'

And he said, 'Oh, I don't believe all that. I don't believe they'd do things like that.'

And McKeon, he said, 'Sir, I'd like to take my pants down and show you the big scars on our backs and bottoms.'

And I said 'That's true, that's what's goin' on.'

Anyway Andrews in the District Court said, 'I hereby sentence you, Alan Edward Fisher, to eighteen months imprisonment, Kenneth James McKeon, here's eighteen months for you, Morgan, you're in too. So long.' The other guy, as you know, Reepsdorf, he's still in the hospital, partially paralysed and he was in there for six to eight months with the injuries. Then Andrews said, 'Fletcher, I sentence you back to Westbrook till you're eighteen or otherwise dealt with.' It was still the same sentence that I originally got in the first place.

I sang out to Andrews then, after it all, 'This is all bullshit and I am not stayin' there!'

So they take us back to the cells and I said goodbye to me mates, I said, 'I'll see you again.' And they were as happy as anything, those three guys, because they was goin' to Boggo Road! Oh, they were as happy as Larry. They said, 'See ya Crowie.'

I said, 'Geez, I'm goin' to get a floggin' again!'

You know Fisher sort of laughed and so did Morgan. They said, 'Well, you'll have to wait till you're seventeen, Crow. Then you can get down to Boggo Road, mate. Do something up there that'll get you to Boggo Road.'

They'd turned seventeen, you see. I was sixteen. And you had to be seventeen to be sent to Boggo Road.

So they took me back to Westbrook and Golledge wasn't finished with me, yet. He said, 'I believe youse were complainin' to the judge and you abused the judge, Fletcher.'

I said, 'Yes Sir.'

'And I believe you were complainin' about your backside.'

'Yes, Sir,' and I just looked at him.

He said, 'Don't look at me in that tone of voice. I'm goin' to give you another floggin'.

Down with me pants again, on top of that other one. Me bum wasn't that sore by then but he really give me another floggin' and ripped me arse all up to bits again. Ripped me back too. He said 'Take his hair off again!' So off goes me hair again. 'Put him on the path.'

Fuck, what had I come back to? What sort of lunatic asylum was this place?

Anyhow there was the same old routine. Admittedly he didn't leave me on the path too long this time; I think I only did about six weeks on the path, then. One day he's goin' off to everybody on Parade and he says, 'Fletcher, step forwards.' I step forwards and he says, 'Now I'm goin' to give Fletcher another chance, but he's not leavin' the orchard, he doesn't get into any other parties. He's got to do that with the diggin' fork in the orchard, just dig, dig, dig. I've got to do this to you boys because I love youse and I want to make good men out of youse.'

The other officers is laughin' to themselves, thinkin' how funny it was, and that's about the end of the story here. It's what happened here.

THE RING OF FIRE

A former resident from this period said that he was aware of sexual abuse by bigger boys and of boys being raped in the shower.

Two witnesses named two smaller boys who were sexually molested by the other boys. ...most of the older boys at Westbrook had a smaller boy who would act as their 'girlfriend' and have to submit sexually. He testified that the officers were aware of this practice.

Commission of Inquiry into Abuse of Children in Queensland Institutions
Leneen Forde AC, 1999.

―――――――――――――

Now regardin' sex in Westbrook.

You must realise that when you went into Westbrook, you were a normal boy. But after a time, maybe a year or eighteen months, you became very hard and your attitude and your ways changed quite considerably. So what horrified and sickened you at first became almost normal. You didn't worry about it. You took no notice.

Most of the bad sexual stuff was put onto the younger boys. Now a lot of these boys were very young schoolboys who were orphans or just unfortunate children whose parents could not look after them properly. It would be done by about twenty percent of the older boys, the toughened-up boys that had been there quite some time.

One of the main places that they had sex with them would be in the bathhouse, in the towel room in the bathhouse. It was only a very small room, about six foot by four foot, where all the towels would be hung on the racks. There was also the back of the Big Rec room, on Saturday nights at the movies.

All this was well known in Westbrook. The officers knew about it, some of 'em were involved in it. They perved on the boys in the shower rooms. The bigger boys would have their 'girlfriends', they'd be school-boys or other boys that were that way inclined, and they would be walkin' around the yard together, even holdin' hands and cuddlin'. They would have their little fun and games whenever they could get the opportunity. Hell-Fire Molly was one boy I remember who was like this and 'she' was beautiful. We all called her 'she' because she looked so much like a girl, you know, soft hair and skin, curves in all the right places and very pretty. She *loved* sex, so you can imagine how popular she was with some of the boys. I don't remember her ever gettin' beaten up. She was the exception to the rule.

So all this was goin' on in front of everybody and no one seemed to care less. When you first seen what was goin' on, you were revolted, but after a while you didn't seem to notice. It was just a normal occurrence.

Later I'll tell you about the time a group of about fifteen of us were sent down to Boggo Road Gaol. We were all put into A Division on the ground floor in cells there, three to a cell, and one of the unfortunate boys there, they used to call 'Grace', was swapped around from cell to cell. The older, tougher boys would be takin' advantage of poor Grace. He'd be in one cell one night with three of 'em and then guys in another cell would pay with some tobacco for him the next night. There was only about ten percent of the boys involved in this, but they were the tougher boys. Boys like Grace might have let themselves be used like this so they wouldn't get belted up all the time.

Any rate, Grace got fed up with this treatment and told a warder at Boggo Road, called Byron Eddy. This Byron Eddy catches two of them with Grace. One of them talked his way out of it, but the other lad, he couldn't get out of it, so Byron Eddy marches this boy to his extreme embarrassment across the compound to the lock-up and puts him in a cell by himself and yells out, 'I'll put you where the dogs won't shit on you!' He was against this kind of thing.

'Shirley Temple' was another one who was used as a sex slave by some of the boys and six different Westbrook boys in Boggo Road were usin' him up, too.

But the schoolboys in Westbrook were the saddest part of the place.

The schoolboys were as young as nine years old, some of 'em. The kids who had nobody outside, they used to wait around the office or near the tankstand after the visitors had left on a Sunday. If somebody got a parcel from home they would offer them sex for some lollies. These were orphans, or boys who had no parcels or anything whatsoever from anybody at all. They had nothing, so they sold their bodies for lollies. This was done outside Superintendent Golledge's office at Westbrook in full view of him and the rest of us.

Some of the screws were doin' it too. Some of these boys, they had their backsides split open and had to go for treatment at the office. Well Golledge would just give them a hunk of cow ointment on their hands to put over themselves. I don't know what was said there. Some eventually ended up in hospital through these sexual practices, but there is no record of any of this.

That time we were put in the compound after we were in Boggo Road, there was an officer who put the word on a bloke called Tommy. Now Tommy was very insulted by this and told Superintendent Sullivan. The superintendent spoke to the officer who then gave Tommy a very bad time in the compound for reportin' this incident. He was drilled unmerciful, but you'll hear about that procedure later.

This same officer was watchin' Boonger Ryan with Grace in the compound. Boonger sang out 'Just like a woman!' and the officers laughed.

My mate Youngie had a similar experience. When Youngie was in the compound, one of the officers propositioned him, sayin' that he could make his life a lot easier for him. He'd let him sleep in the cells and he'd bring him cigarettes and food and lollies and so on. When Youngie refused, he found life a lot harder. This officer was gettin' his mates to put in false reports about him. So there was not much you could do in a situation like this.

Also there was the boys who was sent to the farms to work for farmers on the Darling Downs. Some of these farmers were okay, but there was definitely a pedophile ring which started at the Children's Services, went through the government and involved Westbrook boys and some of the farmers. If the boys came back from the farms before they was meant to, they were given a tremendously hard time back in Westbrook. They got no remission and they just stayed on until they was eighteen. They were really victimised for it. You can work out why. They would not be involved in the 'Ring of Fire'. You've heard the story about Schongie. His story is tragic, nothing less than tragic.

Of course there were good officers at Westbrook who did not like this sort of thing at all, but most of them turned a blind eye to this situation. The smaller, weaker boys were raped in Westbrook, but they didn't dare come forward and say anything.

Everybody seemed to know about it, but nothin' was done about it. I can say myself that I was not involved because I am not that way inclined. It made me sick.

But I have to say this. I don't think you can blame any of the boys involved in this, because after a time, it just seemed normal. But you can imagine how all this affected them for the rest of their lives!

Grace and Shirley Temple are dead now. So are more than half of the boys who were put into Boggo Road.

Leneen Forde has recommended compensation for all the victims of the homes.

But when our cases come before the courts they just get thrown out. The system is rigged against us. And there is all that evidence from the Schwarten Inquiry that was kept from public view. About 1500 pages and 53 exhibits embargoed or disappeared.

SATURDAY NIGHT AT THE MOVIES

'Contrary to the myth, the harsh treatment that was standard in institutions was contrary to the law and regulations of the time. The many beatings and floggings meted out on defenceless children for the most minor misbehaviours should have, if reported, resulted in charges of criminal assault.

Sometimes death resulted. At times, children just mysteriously disappeared after such beatings. Some never returned after being taken away because of serious injury or illness.'

The Enduring Legacy of Growing up in Care in 20th Century Australia
Senator Andrew Murray, 2005

———————

Well Saturday night was probably the night you'd think would be a treat for us, but it always turned into a nightmare. See, you was scared all the time, scared you were goin' to be next. You could never let your guard down. And if you did something really stupid, like laugh, you'd cop it.

After tea on Saturday we'd go back out into the yard for a while then the bell would ring and we'd have to line up double quick and number off.

All accounted for, we'd march off into the wards, there were three of those, and stand to attention at the foot of our beds. Then we'd march down to the Big Rec room.

We sat in straight rows along those long wooden forms and waited till Golledge came down to show us the movie. I don't remember anyone else tryin' to show us a movie. It was Golledge, always Golledge. He liked to have control of everything.

Anyhow, they was old movies, always black and white, and probably made in the 1930s or 1940s. Sometimes we got a more modern one, not often, though.

Now Golledge would always stop the movie when there was a bit of violence. He'd put his hand over the projector when, say, Hopalong Cassidy would start shootin' at the bad guy and he'd tell us, 'Too much violence here!' Then he would give us a lecture about why we couldn't see it.

'Bein' a father to youse all, I have to tell you that's it's too violent for youse,' he'd say.

And that was the end of the movie.

We'd all march back to our wards and go to bed.

On other occasions, the reels of film would get all tangled up and Golledge would say, 'Oh, can't fix it, can't fix it, ' and there'd be this big mess on the floor. Golledge'd be too pissed to do anything about it. There'd be too much plonk in him.

If anyone would be stupid enough to laugh, or even if you laughed at a funny bit in the film too loud, Golledge would go crazy. He'd stop the movie and it'd be on with the lights. He'd grab somebody and it'd be down with his pants. He'd give 'em a floggin' then and there and he would punch into 'em too. He'd mostly go for people in the front row, they were the closest and mostly Aboriginal boys.

We older, tougher boys would know to sit up the back, away from him.

He'd be rantin' and ravin' and everybody would be terrified, not knowin' who would be next. Then that lunatic would explain that he loved us and he had to flog us, etc, for the good of us, to make us into fine citizens. And then, maybe back to the movie, or to the wards and bed.

You never knew when you was goin' to be flogged. You were constantly in fear, 24 hours of the day. Every day. You were on 24-hour alert in your brain. It was the only self-protection you had.

KANGAROO HOPPING

This was a punishment mostly imposed by the warders for minor offences such as talking in line, talking in the wards and talking in the recreation room. Again, this punishment, when imposed, was never entered in the punishment book as required by Reg. 107. It consisted of the inmate, crouched down on his haunches, jumping up and down in a manner similar to a kangaroo's hop. I think the periods mentioned by boys...have probably been exaggerated but I do think that the punishment has been imposed for longer periods than the five minutes claimed by the Supintendent and warder Keates.

Westbrook Farm Home for Boys Inquiry,
Schwarten AE 1961, Queensland Government

Saddler was a drillmaster and the teacher of the little kids. I don't think he was a cat (homosexual), but he was the most sadistic bastard I ever met.

After you'd finished work, before lunch, you had to drill for half an hour. Everybody had to. Didn't matter whether it was 120 degrees in the shade or 10 degrees in a howlin' gale.

I might have mentioned that we only had one set of clothes a week. You had to work in these clothes and you had to drill in them. So after a drill session in the middle of summer, you really stank. And he would drill the arse off you.

Part of the drill session was kangaroo hoppin'. This went on for as long as Saddler wanted it to and depended on what sort of mood he was in.

You'd be fallin' over from the pain in your legs and back and he'd come along and kick and bash you while you were down, especially if you was Aboriginal.

He'd have you runnin' on the spot with your knees up real high until you collapsed. Golledge and his henchmen would be up on the verandah watchin'. Saddler would be showin' off to them.

One day I saw the most terrible bashin', kickin' and punchin' I'd ever seen in my life on a boy. Saddler was into Turbane because he could do no more drillin'. He'd collapsed. He kept on and on at Turbane, who was half-Aboriginal.

This drillin' and bashin' was a daily experience. Turbane got it on a few occasions.

On one occasion Turbane stood up to him. He shaped up to Saddler and Golledge put the gloves on him, on this strong, tall, young drillmaster who was superbly fit, and on Turbane, who was much smaller, exhausted after his morning's work and half-starvin'.

Turbane give him a run for his money, but he still got badly bashed.

After drillin' we'd line up again, number off and then be marched off to lunch and food, glorious food. This consisted of grubs and flies in our so-called stew, plus the two chunks of bread called 'darbs'. There was supposed to be meat in this stew, but you rarely saw it. The officers were knockin' it off. And the bigger boys would be helpin' themselves to the weaker boys' food (which was found by the Schwarten Inquiry to be unfit for human consumption.)

The food improved a bit after the mass breaks, well it slowly started to improve. That was because the screws were frightened to steal our food when the public began to get an inklin' of what was goin' on in Westbrook.

MORE BOYS FROM THE 'BROOK

Ikey Williams, John Chambers and John Munt

Very few children who experienced institional care for long periods or at crucial stages of their development have escaped detrimental effects in later life and this has often damaged their ability to live as effective members of society. Their problems often include low levels of literacy and numeracy, high incidences of alcoholism and sustance abuse, high levels of unemployment, homelessness and imprisonment and poor health. Sadly, suicide rates are comparatively higher than for the general population.

Forgotten Australians
Senate Committee Report on Australians who experienced institutional
or out-of-home care as children, 2004

Ikey Williams' story:

Ikey's real name was Kevin but he only got 'Ikey' at the Brook. He got put in Westbrook for lettin' some horses out of the Rockhampton pound. He was a horse-lover and he didn't like the way they was cooped up in there, or the way they was bein' treated. He got nine years for this 'crime'. He was only nine when he went in.

He was one of the schoolboys and he was supposed to receive schoolin' in Westbrook, but he never learned to read or write. I often wonder about them other schoolboys, too, what they learned in there.

Ikey is Aboriginal. When a copper came round to his place after the horse incident, his mother told him that his father would sort Ikey out when he got home. But the copper said he wanted him charged. So Ikey comes up before a magistrate who says that it'd be best for Ikey to be sent to Westbrook so's he could learn a trade. Ikey thinks his mother had to pay every week for him to stop there.

He was put to work in the dairy for Wensley, 'The Schnoz', we used to call him. Ikey did the milkin' and the other dairy work and he had to get up early each day to bring the cows in. Anyway, most of the screws was pretty racist and they give him and the other Murris a particularly bad time. Ikey said Scotty was all right to him and the bloke who ran the boot repairs, Muller.

Ikey escaped ten times and got ten floggin's.

His Mum and Dad came to see him one time early in his stay there and they were shocked to see the way he looked. He'd had his hair off after a floggin' and they'd ripped his scalp around with the clippers. His Mum went crook on the superintendent, there was a big argument in the office and Ikey's Dad finishes by knockin' Golledge down. That was the end of Ikey's family visits. Forever.

At Westbrook they let you earn money by growin' vegetables and flowers and you could sell them to visitors on Sunday. If you wanted it, you got given a plot of dirt, but you weren't allowed to water it with a hose, it had to be done with a bucket or waterin' can. You were allowed to work on your garden when you knocked off work, or on Saturday afternoons or Sunday. When other boys got released, or if they didn't want to work on their plots no more, they could give you theirs. Ikey finished up with a whole row. He made good money by sellin' his flowers and vegies.

We had to take the money we made to the office and give it in and they would write it up in a book. You was supposed to get the full amount when you left, which we didn't. Ever. Ikey should have been given a lot of money when he left, he got nothing near what he earned.

There was two football fields at the back of the dairy. At Christmas and on the Queen's Birthday holiday, sports were played there. One time Ikey got kicked in the shin and the sore went bad and turned into an ulcer. It didn't want to heal. They put bluestone on it but it only got worse. He had to go to the Toowoomba Hospital three times but it still wouldn't heal, the hole got bigger. In the end he got sent to Brisbane to the Royal. They scraped the bone and done a pinch graft by takin' a bit of meat off the top of his leg and puttin' it on the ulcer. He still has a huge scar on his right leg.

He was released from Westbrook a week before his eighteenth birthday. He was told his father would meet him at the train station at Rockhampton. He got issued with some new clothes and a hat and they took him to Toowoomba and put him on a train to Brisbane.

The first thing he did when the train started was throw that stupid hat out the window. 'Dunno where they got 'em from, nobody wore hats like that. Only boys gettin' released from Westbrook,' he said.

It was a fact that all the boys leavin' Westbrook would first go and buy a packet of smokes. Then, as the train went down the Toowoomba Range, it'd be out the window with the lot, their ports and silly hats. The Range must have been littered with them, at one time.

Ikey told me a story about a bloke in the Brook they called Jumbo Richards.

Now Jumbo had no parents or anyone at all to go to when he gets out of the place. Like all the other blokes, he dumps his port and hat out of the train but when he arrives in Brisbane, he's walkin' around, wonderin' where to go and he notices everyone's lookin' at him because he's wearin' these stupid clothes they give him at the Brook. Magistrate Schwarten said in the Inquiry that the clothes the boys wore at Westbrook were so poor-lookin' with patches on patches, that he never seen such a poverty-lookin' lot.

Well anyway, Jumbo is just a teenage boy and he's embarrassed about his clothes, so he robs a shop for some decent things. He gets caught and is given another two and a half years! He's only been out about 36 hours after doin' three years in Westbrook and he's got to do another two and a half years!

To make a long story short, Jumbo makes use of a sheet that is in his cell and takes the drop. No more Jumbo.

When the train got into Brisbane, Ikey didn't know what to do next.

He didn't know where to go to get the train to Rocky. He went all round the station tryin' to work it out. He couldn't read, see? So he asks a bloke who puts him right and he gets on the train and sits down. Next some other bloke comes along and tells him he's in the wrong seat. Ikey tells him to show him where he should be sittin' and he'll sit there.

The train finally gets into Rockhampton. Ikey looks around but can't see anybody he knows. There was a lot of people at the station and when most of them has gone, he sees a bloke at the other end of the platform. He goes down to him and says 'Are you Mr Williams?' (his Dad)

The bloke says 'Yes.'

'Well,' Ikey says, 'I'm Kevin.'

Ikey got a job at the meatworks as a boner. He was okay until he got on the piss and then he would muck up a bit. He done twelve months in Boggo Road, which included a week in the Black Peter (solitary confinement). Then he was sent to the rathouse, to a place called Sandy Gallop, for continuin' to disobey orders. After this he went to Goodna, an institution for the criminally insane.

This was a really scary place, because, Ikey said, 'They killed people in there.'

After he got out of all these places, Ikey worked on the railways, at Coca Cola and at St Andrews Hospital. He got married to a lovely lady, Bonnie Brady, Pastor Don Brady's sister, and they had a daughter. The daughter has grown up and married now and lives on Palm Island.

When Bonnie died, Ikey kind of lost the plot.

He's a homeless person now, he sleeps in the doorway of St Andrew's Lutheran Church between Spring Hill and Fortitude Valley. He likes 'The Hill' because that was where he once lived with his wife and daughter. He spends his time there or down at nearby Fortitude Valley, watchin' the passin' parade and drinkin' red plonk out of a Coke can. He keeps the bladder of his wine cask in a pond near the church where he lives.

Sometimes a mate will come along and take him home and give him a shower and a feed. But Ikey, like most of us Westbrook boys, doesn't like to mix with too many other people. He is very much his own man.

John Chambers

John Chambers escaped from the Brook five times and a couple of these escapes was quite ingenious. He said they were just spur of the moment things, not premeditated or planned.

One time he crawled through a paddock of barley from the orchard to the main road. They had three truckhorn hooters mounted on posts and they used to set these off when someone bolted. When the wind was blowin' the right way, you could hear 'em in Toowoomba, 15 miles away, sometimes even Drayton. That way the farmers were warned that someone was at large, and the chasers who were boys, the sergeants, would get goin' after him. John was caught with his knees red raw from the experience. He was belted, hair off and on the path, usual treatment.

When you got caught Golledge would stop your family visits for three months. Your stripes would be healed up by then, see?

Another time he stole a car from some workmen at Westbrook who were fixin' the refrigeration. They actually left a big Mainline ute parked with the keys in the ignition! He and another boy, David McDonagh, saw them in there, jumped in and roared off past Golledge's office over the cattle grids, the front garden bed and out through the gate. The screws took off after them in the Dodge ute that belonged to Westbrook.

The Dodge was pretty quick off the mark and not far behind them, but they stayed ahead of the huntin' party until Chambers, who was drivin', took a wrong turn somewhere up near Drayton and found they were in a dead-end street. See it was only a narrow dirt road. Chambers told McDonagh he was gonna aim the Mainline directly at the Dodge and jump out at the last moment, but David grabbed the steerin' wheel and swerved round them. They were caught when they lost control of the Mainline and 'brought to justice' Golledge style.

On another occasion, in Top Square, which was at the back of Golledge's office, where we had little vegetable gardens, a few of us boys dug a hole big enough to take two boys. Chambers and his mate climbed into it with a hollow stick each, so they could breathe. They put paper over their faces and we shoveled the dirt over them and planted vegetables over them and watered the earth down to make it look normal.

They stayed there like that for many hours.

Before tea, at five o'clock parade, we all have to line up and the screws see that two are missin'. When the word gets to Golledge, he and his henchmen come down to parade too.

One of the boys, who was a bit simple, stepped forward and gave Chambers and his mate up. He said, 'I know where they are Sir, they're buried up in Top Square.'

The screws took no notice of him. 'Get back into line, you waster, you idiot,' one of the officers yells, 'or you'll get flogged.'

That night, Chambers and his mate 'rose from the dead'. They got out of the vegie garden and escaped to Brisbane.

Well, they get caught out at Wavell Heights in north Brisbane then taken to the Brisbane watch-house. This is a very secure watch-house, the old Brisbane watch-house. They are put in the same cell upstairs where I was put before I got sent to the Brook.

Chambers had got hold of a little three-cornered file like the ones they use for sharpenin' saws. He had it in his boot, so they missed it when he was searched. For some reason the officer supposed to be guardin' them, wanders off, not imaginin' for a second that anyone can get out of there.

Chambers puts his hand outside through the food trapdoor and picks the lock with his file. He opens his cell door and proceeds to the end of the cellblock where you go into court. Then he picks the lock to the door of the courtrooms and the two of 'em escape through a window and down a drainpipe. This made front-page headlines in the Brisbane newspapers.

They were caught a couple of days later and it's back to Westbrook with old Golledge frothin' at the mouth, waitin' to administer the punishments.

John Chambers lives in Brisbane with his wife and family now, but he says that all that stuff that happened at Westbrook is as clear in his mind as it was when he was livin' it more than forty years ago. He says that memories like that never let you go.

John Munt

Another man who is havin' problems puttin' the past behind him is John Munt.

Now this man is something of a war hero! He was a sergeant in an elite division of the army, the Red Berets, I think it was, and he did three tours of duty overseas; in Malaya, Sarawak and Vietnam. John says that in Vietnam he saw some terrible things, but it was nothin' in comparison with Westbrook.

See, John was institutionalised from a very early age. He was in four homes: Wooloowin, Indooroopilly, Riverview and Westbrook. On his way to Westbrook, his hands were cuffed together for smokin' and the bloke from the Children's Services Department tried to sexually abuse him on the train.

When he got to the Brook he was strip-searched and ordered to bend over a table. One of the officers had a three-foot piece of lawyer cane in his hand and he shoved it up John's backside. 'This is what you're here for,' said the officer.

After about nine months in Westbrook, John was called up to the office and introduced to a visitor who was some sort of politician. Then he was left in the room alone with this visitor.

The man told John that he could get him out of Westbrook, provided he did what he was told. When he told John what it was that he wanted, John was disgusted and refused. He was later flogged for his disobedience.

In Riverview he'd got a bad ulcer on his leg and it didn't want to heal during the time he was in Westbrook. He almost lost his leg over it. He was taken to Ipswich hospital and the doctor there wanted to amputate it. Lucky for John, another doctor tried out a new drug on him. It was called Penicillin and it saved his leg.

He was 'farmed out' at Dayboro and Riverview and at his first couple of farms he was not allowed in the house and had to sleep outside with the animals or under the tankstand and take his meals outside too. Then he was sent to a property near Kulpi and worked for a man called Clive Schmidt who tried to help him. Clean livin' conditions and good food helped heal the ulcer and the hole in his shin began to skin over.

On his eighteenth birthday, Christmas Eve, 1954, John was discharged from the 'care' of the Queensland Government. He left the farm the following February to join the Australian Army. Boys from the homes were expected to join the army and many of them did. See, they was used to bad food and hard conditions and didn't seem to mind army life as much. John had to wait a year before they took him on, though. He had bad ulcers on his legs and was very run-down.

But army life was a breeze to John. He quickly earned the respect of the officers and men and did real well.

Though John Munt was in Westbrook some years before I got there, we'd shared similar experiences and became friends. Westbrook boys have a kind of bond see? So many people don't know what we went through, could never understand or even believe all that stuff that happened to us. But we experienced it and because of that, we know where the Brook boys are comin' from, if you get me meanin'.

John says you can get debriefed when you get back from from a war, but nobody ever debriefed you when you got out of the 'Brook.

THE MASS BREAK-OUT

These regulations (The State Children Act of 1911) give an impression that the primary intended purpose and nature of the institution (Westbrook) was rehabilitative and reformative. However, Westbrook was also punitive in that it was a place where boys were detained for offences against society.

Ryan, unfortunately, was committed to Westbrook at a time of great disorder within the institution. He, along with others, made a number of attempts to escape from the institution, which was then being conducted in a brutal and repressive manner. In consequence of public concern following a number of mass breakouts, a Commission of Inquiry was established in May 1961 to inquire into Westbrook.

Some of Ryan's attempts to escape from Westbrook were successful and while at large he committed further offences. The Westbrook authorities, with the endorsement of the State Children's Department and a panel of psychiatrists, reacted by placing Ryan in the Security Unit of Westbrook where he could be kept under weekly psychiatric observation.

Royal Commission into Aboriginal Deaths in Custody
Report into the death of Vincent Roy (Boonger) Ryan
Commissioner LF Wyvill, 1991

Golledge done me no good deed by putting me in the orchard. I ended doin' about eighteen months in that party. It was on about five acres of land and they had about 30 boys working there, growin' vegetables. You'd dig one garden at one end and then you'd mulch it three times and then you'd go to another garden. You'd dig it up and down, up and down, continuously until Hookey Woods or Seiber would be satisfied the job was done properly.

It was very cold in that orchard in the winter, freezin' cold. It was hot in summer. It was a wide, open space, so everyone in the office could see you.

There was no talkin' allowed, no laughin' and if you were caught stealin' a carrot out of a bed, or any other vegetable whatsoever to eat, you were flogged with this big stick by Woods. It was about four or five feet long and thin, like a big cane. That happened frequent because we were often hungry.

The officers was stealin' our food.

The food for us was becomin' scarcer and scarcer. We were gettin' less and less meat, they was already very small amounts we ever did get, and the good bread was all taken. Everything was taken from the place. The officers would come up at nighttime and take it all.

See, there was several houses on this property and there was several officers livin' in these houses. So they were all livin' off our food. The little bit of milk that we were allowed, that was taken, the butter that was made at Westbrook was taken. So you could see how it was goin' to end as it got worse and worse.

Some of this might have had something to do with Golledge. I've found out since that at one time he recommended to the Department that none of the warders should get a pay rise. Maybe they was dirty on him for that. And took our food as their due.

And the floggin's became more frequent, the public beltin's. They'd get the boys in the big Rec room and one boy at a time would be flogged, screamin' unmerciful, in front of us all. Then off with his hair and out on the path he would go.

So the place started to get very violent. One Sunday night, I remember this very clearly, a lady from a church group came from outside to do a church service.

She was a lovely lady, she had her husband there and two other people. We were in there, singin' 'Rock of ages, cleft for me'. Imagine about 130 guys singin' 'Rock of ages' in this small area, 'cleft for me, let me hide myself in thee. '

A boy had absconded earlier in the day and he had hid in the haystack. The search party was out for him and this service is on at night time, around about seven o'clock and we're all singin' this song and the visitors are bangin' the tambourines and whatnot and then all of a sudden you could hear this blood-curdlin' scream. I'd not heard a scream like this before.

Anyway, from what we could make out of it all, a pitchfork went through this boy because he was hidin' in the haystack. Golledge and his henchmen, they were poking around the haystack with pitchforks. One of them had put the pitchfork through this boy, partly through this boy or right through this boy, we don't know to this day, because we never seen that boy again.

They said he escaped.

You can use your own imagination. Did he escape, wounded, with all those officers around him?

Yeah. I figure I know where he went. Probably down to the long paddock, in the dump or into the silo pit. Or even out near where the grapes was growin'. Golledge hated for you to be anywhere near there, even when there was no grapes on the vine. Somewhere in the grounds of the 'Brook, where all those other missin' children went. That's my take on the matter. And I wonder what happened to Bluey McGaul?

You might ask me about 'all those others'. Golledge later said in his own notes that 'to the best of his knowledge' three boys died during his time at Westbrook. In his own hand, he wrote that one boy died from eatin' grapes. Well, that's a funny thing, isn't it, to die from eatin' grapes?

Another mate of mine, Don Cameron, says he saw a boy climb up onto the tankstand, which was 30 feet high, and jump off. This was somewhere between August and Christmas in 1957, Don said. He pleaded with this boy not to jump. Don said he told Cramp, who was one of the screws, that he was goin' to jump, but nobody tried to stop him. Though nobody knew what they done with him, his body, that is, the belief is that that boy died that day. His body was too smashed up for him to survive. This was before my time at the 'Brook, but I knew about it. We all did. Don had an interestin' take on Westbrook. He'd say, 'Always expect to be abused and humiliated, because that's how it is. And when you're not, it's nice.'

Anyhow, this night, as the screams were comin' from the haystack, the singin' of 'Rock of Ages' which was real loud, became just a murmur.

The woman that came from outside, she started cryin'. She just started cryin'. She closed the whole meetin' and then Golledge came over not long after and she was still cryin'. She was physically shaken by all this and so was everybody else in her church group, visibly shaken by these screams. It was terrifyin' for them. She had to walk out of that church meetin'. She said 'I'm sorry boys, I can't stay, I've got to go. I'm sorry.' And she walked out and she was just cryin'. And Golledge then took over the church meetin'. He done a wonderful job, that day. By the way, those kind people never returned to the 'Brook.

When they'd gone, he came back down and he started singin 'There's a land that is fairer than day, And by faith we can see it afar, For the Father waits over the way To prepare us a dwelling place there.' He said 'I want this song sung.'

So we're all singin' this song. He suddenly stops the song and says 'You!' to one of the dark boys, Turbane. 'You! Yer not singin' properly. Right, up here, pants down.' And he starts floggin' and floggin' him and punchin' him and kickin' him and whatnot. 'Back to yer seat.' Then he grabs another boy and he does the same thing to him.

And then the lunatic would go back to normal: 'Righto boys, There's a land that is fairer than day. ' and on he'd go like a normal person.

Then after the church meeting he would give us a good lecture about how he loved us, he was a father to us all and these floggings must be done so we can go outside into this world and be wonderful young men.

That was the sickness of this lunatic and the sickness of the officers who worked there, who stood by watchin' this goin' on for years and did nothing, with the blessin' of the government.

As I said earlier about the food.

Well, when the grubs started to appear in our food, it was a regular occurrence, eatin' grubs. We tried to complain, but, well, if you complained you was flogged. You weren't game to complain.

More boys were gettin' flogged and they were runnin' away. Every day nearly, someone was runnin' away and they'd be caught and brought back and flogged and hair off, you know, usual treatment, and the path was full of boys, six of seven of us. They had extra paths put in to keep 'em marchin'. And what a sight to see! Young boys, old boys, big blisters on their feet. One boy was made to march up and down with no shoes on. He lost them when he shot through. He took 'em off to run faster and lost 'em when he put 'em over his shoulder. He was made to march up and down with bare feet. His feet were purple, blisters on them and everything. They eventually gave him a pair of shoes.

And the castor oil was being administered much more often because we were hungry and stealin' carrots and anything we could get from the orchard. One boy stole some grapes and had the castor oil treatment in front of us. Golledge grabbed him by the hair and forced his head back, then he smashed the bottle into his mouth, breakin' his teeth, and made him drink the whole bottle. Of course then you'd get the runs something shockin' after this. That particular boy disappeared after this treatment. I think he died. He probably drowned because the oil got into his lungs when he was gaspin' for breath. But Golledge was convinced the grapes killed him.

I never received the castor oil treatment because by this time I was pretty elusive, I suppose. I made sure I didn't get caught. I stole plenty of carrots. Not many grapes, they only used to come on once a year, so I never got many grapes.

So this was the run-down on the place, then.

Fights were goin' on amongst the boys themselves in the bathhouse. If someone looked sideways at you, you'd say, 'I'll meet ya in the bathhouse.' The officers knew what was goin' on and we'd all cram into the bath-house, on the cement floor, and we'd punch it out in there, bare knuckles, until one boy beat the other boy. That was our entertainment. We used to look forward to all these fights in the bathhouse. But it was really sick, that behaviour. It was cruel. It was sadistic.

The only thing Golledge let us have in the yard, they were kept in the office, was the boxing gloves. But the boxing gloves had all the padding on the inside worn out, so it was really bare-knuckle fightin'.

Every once in a while, Golledge sees a couple of boys havin' a scuffle, so he puts them up the office, the officers would all be watchin', and makes 'em wear the gloves. It was wrong, really wrong, because some of the big boys would be fightin' some of the little boys or some of those boys that had only been there a little while and weren't toughened up yet. Us big boys had been there a while by now and we were pretty bloody tough. But the little boys, that hadn't done long in the place, they was the victims of all this. Their time would come, of course, when they'd be tough like us and have no feelin', lose all their feelin'. I might've regained some feelin' over the years, but at that time it was slowly wanin' and the feelin' wasn't much, no more.

And then along come these guys by the names of Dooley and Bird.

I was surprised that Golledge gave them their jobs at Westbrook. He probably thought because Dooley was an ex-boxer and very tall with a pug-nosed face, 'Oh he'll be good, this bloke, he'll knock the wasters down.'

But Dooley was only there a week and he couldn't believe what he was seein'. Couldn't believe it was possible for this to be goin' on. He was amazed at the floggin's and all that was goin' on, him and Bird. They was talkin' up against it and talkin' to us boys. They'd give us a cigarette here and there and they tried to make our lives a little bit bearable when they were on duty.

We used to be so happy when those two men came on duty. We knew we weren't goin' to get flogged and we knew we were goin' to be treated normal when they was on, so we treated them good and did the right thing. No boy was allowed to muck up while these two men were on duty, because they treated us so good.

I'll go into one occasion that happened to me about this time. It was brought out in the Schwarten Inquiry. Photos were taken of my face and other parts of my body but I can't get access to them for some reason. Maybe they've been locked up with the other evidence that the public didn't hear about because the Schwarten Inquiry was closed to the public.

We were up early this mornin' and Bird and Dooley were on. We were in the bathhouse, which was a simple shed with a roof out of corrugated iron over a cement floor. Some of the boys probably were laughin', but not loud, because you wouldn't make too much noise, and out of the blue, Golledge comes along.

Well, I had my hat on and he reckons I had it turned up. I can't recollect having my hat turned up and at no time was I kickin' up any stink whatsoever.

He walks straight in there and as soon as he seen me, he grabbed me. It was all in the inquiry what had happened and he was found guilty of what I'm about to tell you now.

Well he grabbed me by the ears first of all, and ripped the bloody things half out of their sockets and shook me so my head kept bashin' against the tin wall. Then he started punchin' me. When he knocked me to the ground he started bootin' me and thumpin' me. This went on for quite some time until Dooley came runnin' down, the screw, the officer, Dooley, the good man. He came runnin' down from the outside and he said. 'Leave him alone! Why don't you have a go at me, you coward!'

Well this was unheard of in Westbrook, anyone speakin' like this to Golledge! 'Leave the boy alone!' he says.

I was on the ground with Golledge over the top of me. He was bangin' my head into the cement floor by this time, then he ripped right up the side of my face with his nails. But okay, that was the end of that for the time bein', while Dooley was there. He didn't do over any of the other boys, either, he just went back to the office.

Bird and Dooley finished their shift about eight o'clock that morning. So then, when we go to Parade, Golledge calls me out to the office. He gave me about fifteen or twenty stripes and put me back on the path, only this time he didn't take my hair off. He probably didn't want Dooley knowin' about it.

So you can see how bad this place was gettin'. It was happenin' to most of the boys in there, they were coppin' this left, right and centre. Not only me, they were coppin' these floggin's too, these bashin's. Anyway, as I said, Dooley came forward in the Inquiry, and Bird and other witnesses, and Golledge was found guilty of all this.

Golledge denied all this at the Inquiry. He said that I was being cheeky to him. How would you be cheeky to Golledge? The size of him! He was six feet four bloody tall, about sixteen bloody stone, built like a big, bloody monster. Anyway, they took my word and all the witnesses' words over Golledge.

Now you can get a fair picture of what was goin' on here. We're freezin', we're hungry, gettin' flogged more and more and they're stealin' all our tucker, so we all started gettin' together bit by bit and plannin' the mass escape from Westbrook.

Quite a few people had some thoughts on the matter.

They had a gun there with one bullet in it. Once a week one animal was killed, one steer, on the farm. This was to feed us. And one idea was to hit Wensley, the sadistic Wensley with a hunk of four-be-two, get the gun, load the gun, go up to the office and shoot Golledge dead. And a few other boys would attack the rest of them and we'd all escape. But luckily enough, a few of us could see the wisdom of not doin' a wrong thing like this.

Now a bloke called Youngie had his mother come up to visit him. And she gave him the front page of the newspaper, the Sunday Truth, which had headlines which said: 'WESTBROOK NEAR MUTINY.'

Now prior to all this, Dooley and Bird had been leakin' to the papers and the TV stations, what was happenin' here. They knew they were about to be sacked, so they let it all out. So when we held it up and showed everybody, somebody yelled out, 'If it's mutiny they want, it's mutiny they'll get!'

Someone also gave me a box of matches, not many in there, but some, and I hid them. Then we lined up a guy we have to call by his first name, Brian, because he does not wish to have his last name mentioned. Oh well, we give Brian the matches and we planned a mass break-out for that night.

It's a strange thing, practically everybody in the Home knew about this mass break, there was dogs in that Home, people who would give you up to the officers, they was set amongst us. But no one said a word, not one soul!

Keates and Bell were on. They were terrible bloody officers and they would know everything that was goin' on. But they were dirty on Golledge too. They closed their ears. They knew what was goin' on, in my opinion, they knew. One of those men was from a Prisoner of War camp, Bell, and Keates was a sergeant in the army, so I believe, and very hated by the boys. I personally can't say anything wrong about those two, they did nothing to me.

The plan was, we'd wait till after tea, we'd have our tea first.

So we marches in and have our tea and when we come outside we put our boots on.

Then someone sang out, 'Run!'

All the boys threw their hats up in the air, cheerin'. Then they bolted.

They were runnin' in all directions.

Some say there was only 36 went for the escape, but there was 60 or 70 boys runnin' through them fields, everywhere. And Brian ran over to the haystack and lit it up. The haystack was as big as a big house and the flames were leapin' about everywhere. It was almost dark, when this was happenin'. The haystack was like a big beacon.

Unfortunately the next part of the plan didn't happen. Two boys went to the wards to burn them down, but they were caught as they were gettin' under the buildings, ready to light them up.

You can get a pretty accurate picture of this story from the Schwarten Inquiry and Golledge's own version of it, but you don't get the full version of it.

So we're runnin' through the paddocks everywhere and there's Boonger Ryan sayin' in a voice just like Golledge's at the prayer meetin's, 'Come back, boys, come back, boys, I'll give yer more darbs, I'll give yer more darbs.' And everyone starts laughin', you know. And we're runnin'. The siren's blurtin' out and cars are goin' everywhere. In the distance is Westbrook, and it's burnin', burnin'.

Anyhow, we went across country, myself and a few others.

Funny thing, we get to Drayton at night time and there's this ditch in Drayton and a car come past so we jumped into the ditch. And what was so funny, there was half a dozen boys in that ditch already.

Ryan, myself, Youngie, Davies, I can't remember the others, Bully, I think, we got to the Harristown State High School. There was that many police around the place, we could see the cars everywhere, flyin' along the side streets, so we decided to stay at the Harristown High School. It was very bloody cold, I can tell you, that night. Freezin'.

So anyhow, I found an opening to the ceiling in one of the classrooms. We put chairs on top of a table and we pushed it open and we all got up into the ceiling. Prior to that, we got to the rubbish bins and got all the lovely sandwiches that these children dumped. It was unbelievable! And we had plenty of sandwiches, half-sandwiches, half a cake, that sort of thing, and we all sat up there in the ceiling and we had a wonderful time eatin' all this lovely food out of the garbage bin, all of us.

There was six of us up in the ceiling and it got cold. Then somebody says, 'There's a kerosene heater down there.'

Well, up went the kerosene heater. But unfortunately, kerosene can get shaken around and spilt goin' up through a ceiling like this and us boys, not knowin' what could happen, when we turned the bloody thing on, the flames went up and started to hit the top of the roof!

There was boys runnin' everywhere and fallin' through the bloody ceiling. I did stay back and smother that bloody fire; I stopped that fire and then sang out, 'Don't worry, it's all right. I've put out the bloody fire. Come back up to the ceiling or someone will bloody see us!'

So we all got back up into the ceiling.

We stayed there for a day, that night, and until the next night, I think, in that ceiling.

Now we all had to go to the toilet, as you realise, so we did it all up in the ceiling. We shit in the ceiling, we pissed in the ceiling. Try to understand, we couldn't get down and go to the toilet. Anyhow, I feel sorry for the people that had to clean it up. I dunno what they must have thought about the stink when they moved into that classroom! When they went back to school! And the holes made when feet went through the ceiling and the garbage bins up there and all.

Anyway, there was Young, myself, Bully and Davies, to my recollection, and we got into Toowoomba together. Boonger Ryan had gone his way with the other blackfeller. We knew we couldn't have him with us because he stood out like anything, bein' a big blackfeller.

Boonger broke into a dry cleanin' shop, somehow, to get some clothes. And in there was a white suit and a panama hat. He's got no shoes on and he puts this white suit on and the panama hat and he's got some cigars, he's robbed some little joint to get them, and he's headed back to Harristown because there was a lot of bush around there and there's a drive-in movie there. So he started a fire on the hill, layin' back there, watchin' the drive-in movie.

Someone calls the cops and they catch Ryan in his panama hat with his couple of cigars and he's just puffin' away there in his white suit. What a sight to see! You can just imagine. We had a good laugh about that for many months to come.

Well we got ourselves into Toowoomba there. We was lookin' for a car. We grabbed this little Morris and I said, 'We'll go to Dooley's place.'

But we had to find a place to hide the car for the night and we found a spray paintin' factory behind the police station and that's where we hid the car and stayed the first day until we drove out to Dooley's, that night.

Dooley, the good screw, who was our friend who was reportin' all these incidents to the newspapers and everything, he'd told me back in Westbrook, 'If youse get out Fletch, come to my place and I'll help youse out. I'll get you down the Range.'

Because you had to get down the Range, to get out of this bloody place.

We find Dooley's place, he give us really good directions, we get there and I said to the boys in the car, 'Drive down the road a bit, youse park there and I'll get out down here, a coupla hundred yards away from the house, in case the coppers are around here.'

So I knock on Dooley's door and Dooley comes to answer it and he's bloody pale. He says, 'Quick, get in here, quick!'

And it's so good to see Dooley. And we're talkin' about the break and he says 'Look I can't get you out of here. I've checked the Ranges out. There's road blocks everywhere, on all the roads out of this whole bloody area. The whole of Toowoomba is road-blocked off.' He said, 'Look little Crowie, all I can give you is what money I've got here and I'll give you me tobacco and here's a jacket for you to keep you warm. And you'll have to get out of here mate,' he said. 'They're watchin' my house.'

I said 'Okay, Tom.'

So anyhow I gets out of the place. I walks out of the front gate for a start, and I'm startin' to walk down the road to where the car is with the other escapees. And I notice this FJ Holden, it wasn't a police car, and the lights come on and I notice that there are coppers in there, so I sing out, 'Coppers! Go for it!'

Anyhow, I bolted over the fences, ran down through more fences and about a block or so away, I crawls in under this house. It wasn't very far off the ground, but I got right under it, in the dirt. I laid under this guy's lounge room and how I knew it was his lounge room was because there was this big chimin' clock in there that went all night long. The other boys, they sped off, roarin' right through Toowoomba and out along the Oakey Road, because they couldn't get down through the Range.

It's funny that, they probably didn't know where they was goin', and the police cars were roarin' behind them with their sirens blarin'. Oh, they probably knew that they'd had it. So they thought the only way they could get away now, with these police cars behind 'em was to jump out of the car, which they did, and let the car keep on runnin'. Eventually it probably went over a bit of a cliff, or something. But they were caught.

These coppers really wanted us because many squad-car loads of police come from Brisbane to give reinforcements and they were drivin' around the block with a loud-speaker. 'Lock up all your doors, lock your windows, lock your car. There's a Westbrook escapee in this district.' Well they were goin' round and round the block and then eventually about two or three in the morning, they laid off and just disappeared. They thought that I'd broken through the net. Not that they knew who I was, I was just another boy, see.

Anyhow, I was smokin' all night long under there. My hands were bloody black with nicotine the next mornin'. And you could hear the Grandfather clock goin' dong, dong, dong dong, dong, dong, dong, dong, one o'clock, then two o'clock, then three.

I waited till about six in the morning and I knew I had to get out then, I had no food, no water. So I gets out, don't I?

And I'm walkin' along the main road and there's a little shop open and I went in there and bought some cigarettes, some biscuits and milk. I had no shoes on, I can't remember what happened there, I must have left my shoes at Westbrook.

I must've looked a sight, cause I had outside gear on, too, but no shoes and I'm crossin' the road from the shop and I see this great big squad car comin' down the road and guess who I see in it? I see Youngie, Bully and Davies, they're sittin' in it, and naturally the copper says, 'Is this a Westbrook boy too?' when he seen me. And they say, 'Oh no, no, no.' And the coppers didn't even bother pullin' up, they continued on their way to take the boys to the watch-house.

And I'm thinkin', Shit, this was a close call!

So I cross the road to get into a side street which is a dead-end street, but it backs onto the train line, see. I reckoned I could jump the rattler that'd take me to Brisbane from there. The train goes down this bloody big hill at Toowoomba at a snail crawl. And once you got on the train, you'd climb up to the roof of the goods carriages where there was a bit of a hollow thing at the top. That was the way Robin Parnell got away from Westbrook and some of the other boys, too. Jump the train and lie on the top until you got to Brisbane.

I'm half-way along this road and a bloody police car pulls up beside me and a copper says, 'Hey, what's your name?'

I gave him some name, not mine, of course.

He said, 'Are you one of the Westbrook boys?'

I said, 'Oh no, Sir, I just live across the road in that house there.'

'Well lad,' says the policeman, 'we'd better go over there and check you out.'

And I says, 'Yeah, you're quite welcome.'

They're right around me now, three of 'em. So I walks up to the house and knocks on the door and a woman answers it.

I'm carryin' on the bluff and I says, 'Hi Mum.'

And the woman says 'Who are you? I've never seen you in me life before.'

So the police put the handcuffs on me and put me in the car and take me back to the watch-house. They charge me with the illegal use of a motor vehicle.

I was the second-last one caught in that mass escape. One guy got right away. He got to Tasmania. It's in the reports that they caught him in Tasmania, but they didn't extradite him back to Westbrook.

The mass break-out was over the TV, the radio and in the papers. Anyhow the Toowoomba watch-house was full of boys from Westbrook. They maybe had about 15 or 16 of us in there. This can be all verified in the Schwarten Inquiry, reports from the Westbrook officials them-selves and the government.

So we're set to go back to Westbrook.

I can't remember how long we were in the Toowoomba watch-house. I think I asked for a couple of seven-day remands and I got mine. A lot of them didn't get theirs, because they didn't know to ask for them. And there's old Kearney, the magistrate, glarin' at me again.

So eventually, I'm taken back to Westbrook with some other boys, Youngie, Tynan, Bully and them.

We get our floggin'. Not much of a floggin' this time, by the way. We weren't gettin' flogged too hard. You know, Golledge wasn't rippin' our hair off, no more, either. He just gives us a floggin'. He's in shock. The whole joint's half-burnt down. There's too much in the papers about it and the public is screamin' for an inquiry.

By this time the public are on our side.

Now we get to that other mass break that happened. This happened in the Big Rec and only a couple of weeks later.

Al Fletcher and his sister, Denise, aged about six and seven, in their Scout and Red Cross uniforms at the Pickering Street War Memorial, Enoggera, Brisbane.

An article from the Toowoomba Chronicle in which a warder puts his job on the line and supports the boys' allegations of mistreatment.

Fletcher, aged 15, at his one and only visit, standing in front of his cousin's car at Westbrook.

Warder asks why flog decent kids?

Mr. Daly's allegation of brutalities at Westbrook continue:

- Inmates JESSUP and LOWE between them receive. 45 strokes from a heavy bull-hide strap 28 inche. long, for picking grapes from the vines. They wer. then forced to drink a noxious substance and receive. the ignominious horse-clipper haircut.

- Inmate PALL, victim of a bad burning accident, flogged on the accident scar tissue twice with the 28-inch strap.

- State Child LIDDY flogged until he obeyed an order to kneel and beg for mercy.

- Invalid boy PATRICK DALY punched on the face. His glasses were broken and a warder called him a "four-eyed pig."

- Inmate MUNCHER flogged in February, 1961, until blood-stained.

- Colored inmate WILLIAMS flogged and forced to perform humiliating actions.

"15 lashes"

- Inmate TURBAYNE received 15 lashes.

- Inmates ATKINS and KELLY ordered to do three months "on the path" — a punishment track on which they were forced to walk backwards and forwards for hour after hour.

- Inmates STAINES, BUSHELL, RITCHIE and EVANGELLATUS also given the "path" punishment.

- Inmates ABBY and BAKER forced to stand stiffly to attention until midnight.

- Inmate PRICE received 12 lashes at Christmas.

the horse-clipper haircut and was put on the "path" every day for one month.

- Inmates HARTOS, BULLY and McPHEE-SON each received 15 lashes and the ignominious haircut.

"Just kids"

The warder who has joined the chorus of complaints about the running of. Westbrook Home said that of the 130 boys at the Home, about 90 were "decent lads at heart."

"Some of these kids are only 11 to 12," he said. "They are there simply because they are neglected children."

"I'll admit there are some really bad types among the others," he said. "They have got to be handled roughly — it's the only language they understand.

"But as for the more decent type of lad — sometimes they need to be pushed a bit, but not flogged or made to walk "the path" as punishment.

Shivering . . .

The warder said conditions generally at the Home were poor.

Clothing was inadequate for the cold weather. Boys were given cotton shirts and trousers, and a cardigan for the winter months.

In the early morning they were made to stand at attention, for as long

as 15 minutes, shiver. miserably in the cold wh they waited for breakf:

They were made to w. and shower in cold wat even though hot water v available in the tor block.

Meals were poor growing boys, and : properly cooked. A sl of bread, with dripping jam, one sausage in a of gravy, and a cup of was a normal breakfast

"Homesick"

Their boots made prisoners at Boggo R. Jail, were not replaced even when the nails evens through.

He said that there w. dozens of escapes and tempted escapes that one heard about.

"It is my firm be. that the boys escape cause of the treatm. they get and because o: in a while they get hor sick.

"What a lot of : warders don't seem understand is that tl are only kids and it i. natural reaction for th to long for home once a while."

He admitted that . creational facilities "w. not too bad" but were stricted by the ea "lights-out".

The recreational hut h: a billiards table, tab tennis, wireless and sm: library.

He alleged that a "pln system was operating inform on boys as well warders.

"Dodging . . .

Meanwhile in T. woomba the Mayor, Ald-man McCafferty, is a urging a public inqu into Westbrook admin tration.

Alderman McCaffe wants to see over Wc brook himself.

"I have tried seve. times to contact Dr. No for permission, but e. time I have been told is not available," Alderm. McCafferty said yesterd "It begins to look as if is 'dodging' me.

The Dairy. Boys had to work around the farm. This posed photo in the dairy shows inmates once again in clean clothes provided especially for the photographer's visit.

On Parade

The men on the steps are State officials on a visit to Westbrook. The boys were issued clean clothes and bed sheets for the inspection. These were returned to their boxes immediately after the visitors left the centre. Boys said that the officials must have smelled the strong odour of mothballs, even on the parade ground.

Boys were made to parade four or five times a day. When their names were called out they had to reply with their number.

Fletcher is the second boy from the left, facing the camera.

Alan Fisher was one of the strongest boys at Westbrook during Fletcher's time. He elected to escape with his mates rather than serve out his remaining three weeks. He earned another 18 months for his pains.

Queensland Parliamentarian, John Mann, demands enquiry
The MP presents a worn out boot, a length of rubber hose (allegedly used to
beat the boys) and a bottle of castor oil to the Queensland Parliament while
calling for an enquiry into Westbrook in 1961.
Boys who were forced to drink large quantities of castor oil suffered from severe
diarrhoea, vomiting, dehydration and—if it entered the lungs—suffocation.

Ikey Williams and Al Fletcher (Crow) as they are today. Williams often sleeps rough around Brisbane and still can't talk about his days in Westbrook, except to other ex-detainees like Fletcher.

Youth abuse claimed

By RORY CALLINAN

A VIETNAM war veteran is suffering post-traumatic stress from his ill-treatment in a state reformatory more than 40 years ago, the Supreme Court has been told.

Louis John Munt, 59, is suing the Salvation Army and the State Government over the 18 months he spent in the former boys' reformatory of Westbrook near Toowoomba.

A report lodged by psychiatrist Martin Nothling, in support of a plaint seeking damages on the grounds of negligence, said Mr Munt had no recurring nightmares of his experiences in Vietnam.

He said Mr Munt had only a very occasional flashback of his war experiences when he was reminded of the day he found two men "strung up" by the Viet Cong.

But Mr Munt now suffers from lingering post-traumatic stress disorder because of alleged sexual, physical and psychological abuse at Westbrook, according to the plaint.

The plaint says sexual abuse at the reformatory, involved episodes of molestation, sodomy and indecent acts.

The Salvation Army is strenuously defending the action and has applied to have the plaint struck out. It is believed the State Government is also fighting the action.

Mr Munt alleges the Salvation Army had breached its duty of care in allowing him to go to the reformatory where he was molested.

The Salvation Army yesterday said it was strenuously defending the claims.

"The Salvation Army does not have any control and was not involved with the reformatory," a spokesman said.

"The Salvation Army denies any of its staff were involved in any of the acts which occurred at the reformatory and the Salvation Army has applied to have the claim struck out."

Dr Nothling alleges in his report that Mr Munt was told in 1994 that he had been taken from his mother as a child because she was incapable of caring for him.

Mr Nothling said Mr Munt told him of being taken to Westbrook despite having no convictions.

Mr Munt said an officer of the state had taken him to Westbrook when he was 16. He was released when he turned 18 in 1954.

"The plaintiff's head was shaved; he was regularly beaten with a cane; and was subjected to corporal punishment including being forced to walk in circles and perform squat jumps for extended periods of time," Dr Nothling said.

"The plaintiff experienced pain and suffering as a result of this treatment and abuse."

A spokesman for the State Families Youth and Community Care Department Government yesterday said it was unable to comment on the issue because the legal officer involved could not be contacted.

However Dr Nothling said in his report that Mr Munt had written to then premier Wayne Goss about the allegations and received a reply indicating the State Government denied liability.

The matter has been heard before Justice John Helman who has reserved his decision.

John Munt was decorated for service in the Army, including Vietnam, but his nightmares are still of Westbrook.

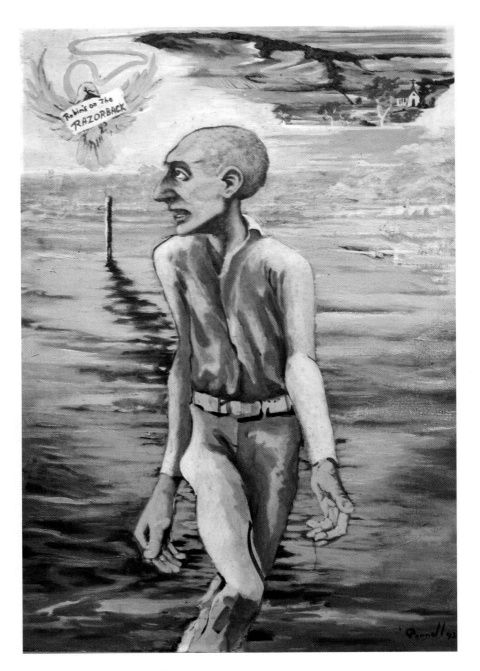

Robin's On the Razorback by Robin Parnell.
Parnell painted these three images of his time in Westbrook. This image is of a
shorn Al Fletcher 'walking the path' because he might have known of Parnell's
escape plans. The Razorback refers to the ridge of hills overlooking Westbrook
and Toowoomba, where Parnell was hiding.

'*Ooh Sir*' by Robin Parnell depicts Al Fletcher being flogged by Superintendent Golledge. Detainees had to scream out 'Ooh Sir' with each stroke or suffer even more punishment.

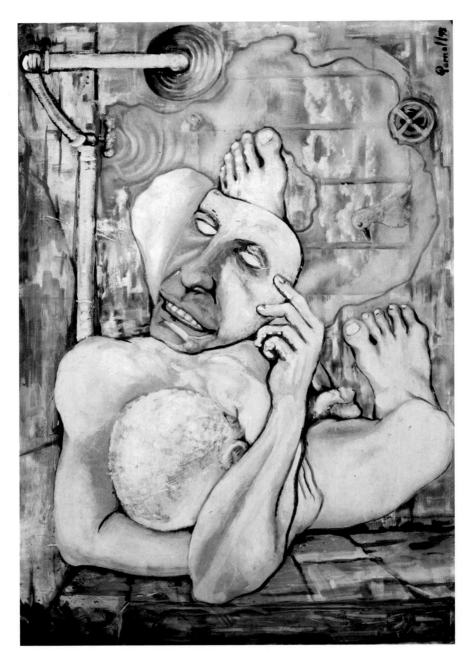

The Shower, by Robin Parnell, is the artist's interpretation of his emotions in the shower block at Westbrook.

THE SECOND MASS BREAK-OUT

Nobody bothered to inquire why children continually ran away. Those who reported abuse as a reason for absconding, especially to the police, were simply not believed and returned to the institution—usually to be summarily punished.

Forgotten Australians
Senate Committee Report on Australians who experienced institutional
or out-of-home care as children. 2004

We staged a fight at the back of the Big Rec as a decoy. The officers thought there was a fight goin' on and didn't take too much notice. But we were actually kickin' out the side louvres. Suddenly we managed to smash enough to make a big enough gap and we all piled out of there, probably about thirty-six of us.

Well, once again, we get into Toowoomba and it's freezin' cold, and I mean freezin', and I'm with Bushnell and a bloke called Evangelatis who was extradited back to Greece in later years. Bushnell, I heard, got pretty high up in the army.

For some unknown reason, I didn't have a shirt on, so I took one off a clothesline we come across. And we're marchin' through the bush and we run into the old Toowoomba Range track that was probably made a hundred years ago. And I said to Bushnell, 'We've found the track out of this bloody place, the old Range track.'

So we walk all the way down there, to the bottom of the Range to a place near Grantham, I think it was. It was cold, very cold and we were freezin'. We'd been on no food, no water even, for a couple of days and it was bloody freezin' down the bottom of the Toowoomba Range.

I said to Bushnell, 'What are we going to do? We'll be stuck down in the bush at the bottom of the Range now, there's no cars we can get down there.'

Evangelatis said, 'Look, let's hitch-hike with one of them semi-trailers.'

It was very dark by now, so we get on the side of the road. This semi-trailer pulls up and he must have been in it with the coppers because right at the back of the semi-trailer was a police car, with its lights off, huggin' the back of it.

It was me that sprung the police car. I said, 'Go for it! Police!'

There was a barbed-wire fence, but I go straight over it. Bushnell and Evangelatis were caught, there and then. But I kept runnin', fallin' over and goodness knows what. And as I'm runnin' they're shootin'. I hear Bang! Bang! Bang!

They weren't shootin' at me, I'm pretty sure of that, just tryin' to give me a fright. And they did give me a fuckin' fright. I'm sixteen years old, remember.

I've got no shoes on and I fell into this big bloody lake or dam, I don't know what the bloody hell it was doin' out there. Anyway, I swam across it and got on top of a hill.

The police didn't leave there. They gave Bushnell and Evangelatis cigarettes and sandwiches, they had plenty of sandwiches because they were out for the hunt for us all night. Apparently we were the last three that were left, in the second mass break.

And they used this big loudspeaker and they sang out my name. They said, 'Fletcher, give yourself up. We're goin' to wait here. We've got you surrounded. Come down here, we got cigarettes and food and you'll be nice and warm. '

I was up this bit of a hill in the pitch black and I said, 'Go and get fucked! I am staying where I am. I am not going back to that lunatic asylum!' And I could hear Bushnell and Evangelatis, in the heavy, cold, night air singin' out, 'Good on you, Crow! Fuck 'em!'

The coppers stayed till maybe two in the morning, with the boys there. They made up a fire on the side of the road, got some sticks and whatnot. The coppers are standin' there, gettin' warm, the boys are hand-cuffed to the inside of the car.

Anyhow, they're gorn the next mornin', but what a cold night! I was frozen! Honestly, my legs were like blocks of ice from the knees down. I'd laid there all night and I'd pulled out some grass to cover me, but it didn't help much. And as the sun rose on the horizon, I knew I had to get out of that area.

I could see the road to Brisbane from where I was, so I followed it, but travelled parallel with it under cover of the bush.

After many hours of walkin', I became exhausted and I lay down besides this creek. I drank plenty of water from there and I got onto some old corn, but it was as hard as a rock. I couldn't even chew the bastard, and I had good teeth, so I thought if I soaked it for an hour it would soften up. But not to be.

So I crossed the road and kept on goin' through the bush, goin' further inland, then crossed it again until I eventually came to the outskirts of Helidon. I knew there was a train station at Helidon. There was also this old bridge near the train station there, so I made for it. Then I lay down on the ground under the bridge and went out to it, like a light, the lovely sun on top of me, warmin' me and makin' me feel drowsy.

I woke up hearin' a train comin'. I jumped up, thinkin', This is it, this is it! I'll always remember this, it was a Friday afternoon.

There was an old shed at the back of the railway station, so I walked into that and found some old lanterns, the kind railwaymen used, you know, the red ones and the green ones. So I grabbed one in each hand and walked up to the back of the train and no one took no notice of me with these lanterns, probably thinkin' I was a worker, or something.

Then I got at the back of the train in between the two last carriages, threw the lanterns underneath it, and climbed up between the two carriages. I stood in there and the train took off. Toot! Toot!

And I thought, Beauty, I'm on me way.

On these trains they used to have a little ladder that went up to the roof. Well, I'm climbin' up that, just as we left Helidon station and of all things, I'm caught by the ticket inspector as I'm on the last rung of the ladder.

'Hey, come down here, you,' he says, 'come down here. You got no ticket, come down here.' He knew.

I gets down there and I says, 'Look mate, forget about me, eh?'

And he says, 'Oh no, you're the Westbrook escapee, aren't ya? It's all over the front pages of the newspapers.'

'Look,' I say, 'can't you forget you even seen me?'

He says, 'Nah. Nah, I can't. They know you're on this train.'

I says 'How would they know I'm on the train? I just got on it.' Anyway they probably knew, somehow or other, I was on there.

He give me a couple of smokes but I wouldn't come inside the carriage. I said, 'I'm stayin' here, I'm not goin' inside.' You see the train was packed with people, probably comin' home from work, and I looked such a bloody mess.

The train was jam-packed full of people, it's Friday afternoon and it was goin' full steam ahead on its way into Gatton.

I was feelin' dreadful. I was cold, hungry and cranky with meself for gettin' caught again. What's goin' to happen to me? I'm thinkin', I'm caught again.

Before you get into Gatton, there's this big railway bridge you come over and I thought, Fuck this, I'll jump straight off this train, off this bridge, one big dive, because there has to be water under this.

So I'm gettin' meself ready to do this, it really had entered my mind to jump, but anyhow, I didn't, thank goodness! Shit, I would have been dead. It was a hell of a bloody big jump and there was hardly any water in that hole, anyhow!

As we're approachin' the outskirts of Gatton, I'm thinkin' of ways to jump off the train, but the train was goin' too bloody fast. And as we came into Gatton, all I could see was police. There was police everywhere.

So, the train pulled up, the police were there, and I got off the train.

But a funny thing happened. There was a lot of young people there on that train and they were all singin' out, 'Good on yer! Good on yer!'

to me and applaudin' as I walked past. Some older people were in it, too. It was a strange situation. I'm walkin' along the platform with the cops all round me, like some hero, or something. People are cheerin' me!

Well the police put the handcuffs on me and walked me right down the end of the station. Then the station master who had his own house there, he came forward and he said, 'Look, before you take him to the watch-house, let me feed this lad.'

The cops were all right, they said, 'Yair, righto,' and took the hand-cuffs off.

So the station master took me up inside his house, the police stayed at the front of the house and at the back of the house, and he gave me cake and some sandwiches and a hot cup of tea. He was a man, that man. I'd love to see him today and thank him.

Anyway, it was all over. Most of the police came down with me and they handcuffed me and the police sergeant said, 'Oh, take the handcuffs off him. He couldn't run if he wanted to. He's had it. Look!'

There was a couple of big burly cops beside me so there would be no point in me runnin', and I said, 'I'm not runnin'.'

The sergeant said, 'How'd you like to go back to the watch-house, by the police car, or would you like to walk back and we'll get yer some pies and cigarettes on the way, eh?

I said, 'That's a good idea.'

There was one of those little pie stands on the side of the station that sell pies and cigarettes. The police just walked me through and the sergeant said 'Oh, what are you smokin'?'

I said, 'Craven A.'

'Well, what do you want?'

I said, 'Just give me a large packet.'

So they give me a large packet of Craven A and bought me some pies and took me to Gatton police station.

Now I'll never forget this. I don't like the police, I can assure you of that, but you must give due credit. They never hurt us Westbrook blokes. They knew what was goin' on in that bloody place.

The sergeant at Gatton, he said, 'Get some warm water and put some salt in there and we'll bathe his feet.'

My feet are all red raw by now, I mean I've been walkin' some forty or fifty mile across country, through the bloody bush on bare feet! And they bathed me bloody feet and they give me a towel and then they said, 'Well, we've got to lock you up in a cell, we're not takin' you back today. We'll take you back tomorrow.'

Well, a funny thing happened here. They lock me in the cell, give me the cigarettes and all, plenty of food, and I just laid on that bloody bed in there and I slept. I was exhausted and had it.

When I woke up in there, early that next morning, I discovered to my amazement, that the cell door was wide open! It was bloody open! One of them bloody policemen opened that bloody door during the night and just left it bloody open for me to go. But I'm tellin' you the truth, I couldn't even get off that bed. I was that exhausted.

Anyhow, a bit later the next morning, it was shut again and some police came in and they said, 'Well, we've got to take you back there, son, back to Westbrook.'

The took me to the watch-house, I was charged with stealin' a shirt valued at one pound, seven shillings and six pence.

Kearney was on again. You could see Kearney was by this time totally fed up with me. He was talkin' very sternly and carryin' on.

So I goes back to Westbrook.

THE SCHWARTEN INQUIRY

Mr Schwarten reported on the many complaints made by the inmates. Criticisms were made of the deficient clothing, poor standards of food, crowded, cheerless dormitories, inadequate hygiene and excessive drill. Punishment, however, was the issue that provoked the greatest number of complaints. Indeed, almost half of Schwarten's final report was devoted to the institution's punishment practices.

'The strap was excessively used, was over severely used, punishment for breaches of discipline was unduly harsh and excessive, there was inequality of punishment and uneven justice. ... inmates were physically assaulted by the Superintendent (Golledge) and certain warders and the schoolteacher in a manner that was vicious and brutal.'

Commission of Inquiry into Abuse of Children in Queensland Institutions
Leneen Forde AC, 1999.

Golledge didn't belt me so bad. Apparently he was told to lay off, not to touch any of us kids no more, because this was hittin' the headlines in all the newspapers. The public was screamin' for enquiries into the place and it was on TV. I find out later that there was a man at the bottom of the Range huntin' for me on horseback, so there was police on horseback.

I only got about ten stripes with me pants up. So they were startin' to flog you with your pants up, you know, not on your bare backside, because the government was shittin' themselves. The whole truth was comin' out by now.

An inquiry was set up by Magistrate Schwarten. In this Inquiry, some of us had enough guts to come forward and give our grievances. I went forward and told them everything I possibly could about this hole we were livin' in and what they were doin' to the kids. And they took photographs of my face and other parts of my body where I was ill-treated.

Bird and Dooley had a little bit of money and they hired a solicitor to represent us in this inquiry, but they could only afford to pay for a couple of days. They went on the national TV saying the boys should be represented by somebody. The government gave us no representation whatsoever, whereas Golledge and his henchmen had all the top men, you know, Drummond and Sturgess, the stars, the solicitors and the barristers comin' up. Their barrister was Jack Aboud, a very well-known legal man who was on the government's side and we had no one. So they just tried to make bloody liars out of us all.

Well, on one of the days of the inquiry, I had been in there for quite some time and they sent me outside to have a break. While I was outside, one of the guys from the kitchen came up to me. See, we were sittin' on a stool outside the kitchen area which was near the Big Rec where the inquiry was bein' held. There was quite a lot of people involved in this inquiry, you know, girls on typewriters, the lot. Anyway this bloke from the kitchen said, 'You know Crow, the bloody grubs are in here again, the grubs are in our food, now.'

I said, 'Okay, get me a big load of them. I'll take them in and show 'em.'

Anyhow, he gets me a big load of the grubs and I go back into the inquiry. And this Jack Aboud, during one part of the proceedings, says to me, 'I suppose you're going to complain about the food, too.'

Now I had all this in me pocket, in a little glass, all the grubs. And I said 'Oh yes, I sure am!' I said, 'We're gettin' fed grubs in here. They're stealin' all our food and feedin' us grubs.'

And he said, 'Oh you're a liar, Fletcher. You're making this up.'

I said, 'No I'm not.' I said, 'Magistrate Schwarten, could I show you the grubs?'

He said 'Oh, by all means, boy.'

So I gets up and I walks up to his desk and I pours the grubs out, the weevils and maggots and whatnot, from the glass, in front of him.

And he says, 'Oh,oh,oh! Good gracious me! Oh, get them back into the glass!'

So I scooped them back into the glass and then Aboud started saying that I got them out of a dead beast down in the paddock and nobody could believe a word that I said.

But Schwarten didn't. He said, 'Where are the grubs now, in what section?'

I said, 'The grubs are in the kitchen, right now, Sir. If you were to leave here now, you'll spring 'em, you'll catch 'em right in the act. They're all in the kitchen now.'

So Schwarten says, 'Righto,' and he closed the inquiry for twenty minutes, or whatever it was, and they had a look.'

So off they all march into the kitchen. And they came back again and called me back in and they had a discussion about the grubs.

Then Schwarten says, 'I hereby find the food unfit for human consumption!'

Aboud jumps up and he says, 'I want this all analysed. I still want this all analysed. I still reckon this is a trick of Fletcher's. This is a trick!'

Schwarten said, 'It's not necessary, but we will have it all analysed to verify.'

It was all analysed and it did verify that all I was sayin' was the truth. The food was certified 'unfit for human consumption'.

This Schwarten Inquiry went on for a long time. It was mostly held in Westbrook and then they closed it down there and moved it back into the city of Brisbane.

The homosexuality in there was brought out with the officers and a terrible lot of other things was brought out. But it was closed to the public. It was a closed Inquiry, even though the public demanded an open Inquiry. So the truth was not brought out and told to the people.

And most of the wicked things of this Inquiry have been put away till about the year 2025. So the public will never know the real truth unless they wait around till then. And who'll remember Westbrook then?

That's the whole idea, of course.

BOYS IN BOGGO ROAD

It was little wonder that some former residents expressed the view that to be sentenced to an adult prison was a relief after the harsh regime of Westbrook. One witness said: 'Boggo Road, compared to Westbrook when we were children, was like going to a holiday resort.

Commission of Inquiry into Abuse of Children in Queensland Institutions
Leneen Forde AC, 1999.

Anyway, as time went by, all the boys with charges were taken back into the Toowoomba watch-house and Kearney remanded us to Her Majesty's Prison, Boggo Road Gaol for four months. They wanted to build a high-security compound in Westbrook. Something no one would escape from.

So we're all there, in the watch-house, the whole lot of us, Boonger Ryan, Tiers, Bully, Ides, Chambers, Grant, Kelly, Holmes, Curtis, and a few others. And we're happy as pigs in shit, oh, we were so happy, we were goin' to Boggo Road. This was better than Westbrook, this was, this was beautiful!

So a black maria comes this mornin' and they handcuff us up and put us inside. And we're on our way to Boggo Road. We didn't get a drink of water, we didn't get a sandwich, they give us nothing. And we were young boys and we're so excited and we're makin' a bit of noise in the back and every now and again, the copper drivin' this black maria would jam the brakes on real hard, and we'd all go smashin' forward and whatnot. They didn't stop to let us go for a piss or to the toilet, so we just pissed through the grill, you know. And every time we went through a little town, we'd make a lot of noise, which didn't make the coppers very happy.

Well when we arrived at Boggo Road Gaol, it was night time. There was reporters everywhere and flashes of light goin' off and bloody TV cameras and we're into A Division.

There's two Divisions in Boggo Road, A Division and No 2 Division, so we went into A Division.

We went through the double gates and they pulled up the black maria. Out we were bundled. We were met by a guy there by the name of Hogarth. He was a three-pipper, one of the highest in the gaol.

He got us all out and he read out all the charges, illegal use of a motor vehicle, stealing, whatnot, whatnot, and he started giving us this big lecture in his big, deep voice.

'Now you lads, you're in here in Boggo Road Gaol. You'll find this much different than Westbrook. You will not be escapin' from this gaol. We are goin' to treat you like we treat all other prisoners. There'll be no mercy for youse and any trouble, you'll go straight into the lock-up.' He went on and on.

Well, I don't know how they ever sent us to Boggo Road because it was highly illegal to put juveniles in there. But I believe that 'Bagman' Jack Herbert, the guy that was in the Fitzgerald Inquiry with Lewis and them and who only recently died, was workin' for the Department at the time. He was behind this sendin' us to Boggo Road Gaol, while they built a security compound to hold us back in Westbrook. Something that we could never escape from. We'd showed 'em up see, by escapin' and complainin' at the Schwarten Inquiry, so the government were out to square up.

They put us on the Ground floor in A wing. There was one lot of cells on one side and they put us three into a cell. It was pretty disgusting. We had a shit bucket in the corner, they locked us up from about three-thirty in the afternoon and you didn't get out until eight-thirty or nine o'clock the next morning. They had one bunk in there so one slept on the bunk and the other two slept on the bloody floor, plus that awful shit bucket in the corner stunk all night. That's what we had.

But it was still better than Westbrook, it was great. We had a cigarette, the food was better and no one was bashin' ya, so we were all quite contented.

For the first two weeks, during the day, they locked us at the back of the surgery and kept us away from all the other prisoners. That only lasted for two weeks, and maybe not even that, I think it was closer to a week. The public was told that we were kept in a special section of Boggo Road Gaol, away from all the other prisoners. But this did not happen after that first week. For then they put us into No 6 Yard, that was a yard on its own with other yards close by that housed the other prisoners.

A gaol is a very public place. There is no privacy when you go to the toilet or when you take a shower. We used to shower in No 6 yard in full view of everyone. Can you imagine what some of the perverts in that gaol were thinkin' with all these fresh young boys runnin' around the place? They used to stand on the 2nd or top floor to watch us takin' our showers. It was like Christmas to them, or a performance of Les Girls.

Well the other prisoners were always droppin' cigarettes over the fence to us and bits and pieces. Everything went along all right for a while and then I wanted to be in a cell on my own. There was startin' to be some trouble goin' on with the other boys, fightin' mainly, in that confined space we were in. Everybody was gettin' on everybody else's nerves. So I went to the Superintendent and asked him if I could be in a cell on my own.

He started ravin' and rantin' and he said 'You should be in with the other boys.'

I said 'I don't want to get into no trouble.'

He said. 'Oh, you're the ring leader of this whole bloody situation, you're the one that started the whole bloody Inquiry!' But he did give me a cell on me own. The Super made sure the cell was right beside the kitchen, the worst place in the whole bloody gaol, but anyhow, I just wanted to be away from everybody else.

I made good friends with Squizzy Taylor. His name really was Taylor but the other inmates called him 'Squizzy' after that bloke in Melbourne. He was always under lock and key and double escort, wherever he went. He was a great big bloke and always closely supervised, but there was this prisoner who had the job of the gaol sweeper, who used to chuck off at him, call him a cat and that, but from a safe distance, of course.

Well one day, this sweeper got too close to Squizzy. It was when the double escort had arrived to take him somewhere and the sweeper's there, callin' out all these insults to Squizzy. Taylor just breaks free from the escort and goes the sweeper. He broke his broom in half and I reckon he broke the sweeper in half, too.

Stopped him from chuckin' off, after that. The sweeper went very quiet after that incident.

I'd still go down to the Six Yard during the day, and one day I noticed some of the wire was loose there. I used to sneak out between the big walls of the gaol and the yards, which was a track right around the gaol on the inside, and I'd go into one of the other yards and I'd get my tobacco off my great mates Graham Cannon and Jim Nicholls that was in there. They'd give me tobacco and I'd whiz back. The guards would be on the wall with the guns and I'd wait till they'd be at one end and I'd rush through. Then I'd wait until they'd be at the other end, and I'd rush back. But unfortunately, this day, I got sprung and the guards pointed their guns at me and told me to freeze. I told them I was just getting tobacco and they told me to get back in the yard. So I get back in the yard and I was then put up to the Superintendent. Unfortunately it was reported in the newspapers that I attempted to escape, another front page, which was all bullshit.

But anyhow, it suited the Superintendent then to get even with me. He said 'You're the one who went to the Inquiry, you're the one that's dropped the bucket on 'em. I'm goin' to fix you up, we're goin' to break you!' He said, 'March him across the Compound into the Back Peter.'

So they took me down into the Black Peter. That's where you go twenty-five steps down under the ground and it's pitch black. And they only locked me in there four or five hours, but shit! I don't know how you could do weeks and weeks in there because you'd go bloody insane. I've heard some blokes did months down there!

Then he brought me out of there and I went back with him to his office and he started screamin' and carryin' on and he said, 'I'm goin' to put you in Number Two Division, in the Bird Cage.

I'd already done a couple of seven-day lock-ups by then. That's locked up in a cell in solitary confinement for seven days on half-rations. One was for fightin' with Tiers, I can't remember what the other one was for. The worst feature of it was you were not let out for a shower for the whole seven days, or even a wash. This was against regulations, by the way.

The Superintendent screams out 'March him over!'

The whole gaol is lookin', I'm only a boy and I've got me swag, which is bugger-all, and they march me over with two prison officers, handcuffed to one on each side, to Number Two Division. And they put me in a cell, into the Bird Cage.

Now all the prisoners in Number Two Division were doin' seven to ten years, you couldn't get into that Division unless you were doin' that long, at least seven years, and they were amazed, seein' a young boy, sixteen, thrown in amongst murderers and goodness knows what else. Halliday, the notorious escape-artist and murderer, he was in the Bird Cage beside me and I was talkin' to him all the time.

The Bird Cage was about six foot by four foot and they had about eight of them in a row. And it was all thick wire, over the roof and every-where. They ended up takin' Halliday out of the Bird Cage and put him elsewhere. Now how it used to work out in this Bird Cage was I'd be double hand-cuffed, that's a hand-cuff on each side of me and an officer each side of me. At about three-thirty they would march me back into my cell, I'd be strip-searched and there was a mat put on the ground, that was what I slept on, and I was on half-rations. There was no ciga-rettes, no nothing, but the prisoners in there was always walkin' past and poppin' me in a cigarette and a match and a striker, which is a part of a matchbox, so I was still gettin' the odd cigarette. And I truly didn't mind it, I wasn't gettin' beaten up and it was still better than Westbrook.

Anyhow, the cells were very small and in the morning all the other prisoners would be marched out first and they'd go and do their jobs and their chores and I wouldn't be taken out for a wash or anything, until about eight-thirty in the mornin'. Sometimes much later.

Two officers would come and march me down to the Bird Cage and I'd have a wash down there. Ninety-nine percent of the officers were good to me, they'd give me tailor-made cigarettes and tell me not to be in any hurry. But they had to do their jobs. They just thought it was disgustin' what was goin' on in there. Then they'd put me back in the Bird Cage. You had a stool to sit on and you'd sit there till lunch time and then back to your cell again before the other crowd of prisoners came over from the workshops. And this was my daily routine. All you could see was a guard with a gun on the tower. The only entertainment you had was the radio on until eight o'clock at night. That was all. I was in the Bird Cage for roughly six weeks.

While I was in Number Two Division there was a terrible suicide I seen. It isn't a nice sight to see when someone hangs themselves. They lose control of their bowels and bladder, shit comes out of them, the piss comes out of them. How I seen this, was I got on the shit bucket and looked through the little peep hole when I heard noise comin' out of that Division, and I seen him hangin' there. And then them bringin' the body out.

Superintendent Smith used to get great delight in comin' over to see me. Well, after a while I don't know if it was great delight, I think he was gettin' a little bit embarrassed. He'd come over there each mornin' and he'd say. 'Have you had enough?'

I'd say, 'Oh, I don't mind it in here, at all, you know.'

And he'd just start ravin' on. What he's goin' to do to me, if I get sentenced back to Boggo Road Gaol. One day he threatened to fuckin' murder me! I was sixteen.

He said, 'When you come back to Boggo Road gaol, if you do get sentenced, you are goin' to spend your whole time in this Division, here, in the Bird Cage.' And he said, 'I'll let you know something else. A lot of the prisoners here, they die. They've died from here. And we put it down as suicide. They fall off that top wing in there, where you are. As you realise, that's three storeys high.' He said, 'They have an accidental fall.'

Now, I thought this was just incredible. Here I am, I've done nothing seriously wrong, all I've done is gorn to the Schwarten Inquiry. I told the bloody truth, I stood up for what were my bloody rights and here they are, threatenin' to murder me!

One day he came roarin' over and he brought Alex Tiers, an Aboriginal boy with him. Apparently Tiers got up to something and Smith said, 'Guess who I'm puttin' in here. Your so-called good mate Alex Tiers.' He must've knew that I was always in punch-ups with Tiers and I was very amazed. He said, 'You're gettin' out, now.'

So he took me out, and they put me back in Six Yard. Tiers was put in there, in the Bird Cage, and unfortunate for Tiers, it really knocked him around. Bein' an Aboriginal, they can't take these confined spaces as much as a white man can. It wrecked him mentally. Eventually they let him out too, but it wasn't much later after that that he died, very young.

Back in Six Yard, one day my name is called out. I had to go up the office and there was Alan Fisher, McKeon and Morgan. The officers told us to get dressed and we get dressed. They had us all handcuffed up and they put us into a police car and they took us into town to the Inquiry, which was being finished off. It was already finished in Westbrook but it was the end of the whole Inquiry and it was bein' wrapped up somewhere opposite Roma Street railway station, in one of them big buildings there.

Well, as they march us in, the warders and the police, Schwarten said 'Take those handcuffs off those boys. They've done nothing wrong to be in here.' He'd changed his tune, this day.

Anyway, they asked us a lot of different questions about what had happened and they went over a lot with us. Schwarten said 'Let those boys sit down the front with their handcuffs off, they're not here being charged with anything. They've done nothing wrong. Take them off.'

So they took the handcuffs off us.

Anyhow, that was it, the end of the Schwarten Inquiry and we were sent back to Boggo Road. That was the last time I saw Alan, McKeon and Morgan for a while. They were in a different section as they'd been sentenced to gaol by now, doin' their eighteen months.

There was a lot of things went on in there. Quite a few of us were locked up for seven days in cells on our own, on half-rations and on mats.

Anyhow this morning, no one knew what was going to happen. No one had an idea. (I can see now why they probably had it in for me, I probably was a bit of a scallywag.) See, they get us out of our cells about four o'clock one mornin', the whole lot of us 'Brook boys. And they march us over to the shed where you get dressed up and we had an early breakfast. Then they told us. They said 'Youse are goin' to court, today.'

We thought, Oh shit, this is it. We're goin' to court. This is it. What's goin' to happen?

I'm hopin' I'm goin' back to Boggo Road. We all are.

But we're not.

They did a psychiatric report on us all while we were in there. And the psychiatrist's report on me was: It would be better to leave him in Boggo Road, he's happy here. My advice is, that if you send him back to Westbrook, he's going to escape again, so it'd be better to leave him in Boggo Road. That was the psychiatric report upon myself. I don't know what the psychiatric report was on others, that is their own personal business.

So we're all dressed up and the big black maria pulls up and we're put inside it. This is about five o'clock in the mornin' and the prisoners are still in their cells. Old Garbage Guts Hogarth was there, that's what I used to call him, naturally not to his face, I wouldn't be game to. Hogarth used to sing out with this big voice, Back, back, left, right, into there. He said to us, 'Youse'll know it when you're sent back next time. Youse'll know it.'

Anyhow, I did end up by callin' him 'Garbage Guts Hogarth.' And I just kicked the side of the van a little and before I knew it, all the boys in that black maria started kickin' the van too and carryin' on. There was really a lot of noise goin' on. And it started the whole Division off. The whole of A Division then went into a riot, hittin' their pannikens against the bars and goin' right off.

I'd kicked the whole place into a bloody riot, unfortunately.

So the maria goes through the gates, and the media people must have had a tip off because they were all there waitin' with their cameras. There was reporters and TV people. And they took us to the Supreme Court building in Brisbane. We were put in the cells there for quite a long time under the old Supreme Court. The cells used to be downstairs. That's where we went.

They took the boys up so many at a time. Some never ever came back down. We didn't know then whether they were released or what, but Chambers got released and Bully got released. They just released 'em, they didn't send them back to Westbrook.

My turn come with Youngie and a few others.

It was me old mate Andrews, the Judge.

He said 'About this terrible carrying on early this morning in Boggo Road Gaol, the riot. ' He went on about the noise that was made and everything. 'You're the ring-leader, Fletcher!'

I said, 'Well we didn't mean it to end up like that.'

He said, 'Anyhow, even if you weren't, I'm having you sentenced back to Westbrook for two years straight. You can't get out for two years.'

I said to him, 'Sir, I'm not gonna stay there. I should never have been sent there. I should never have had to go through all this.'

Andrews said, 'You will be staying there. Since you've been away, in gaol, we've built a security compound in there that you will not be able to escape from.'

I said, 'I am not stayin' there, I'm gonna break out of there. I'm gonna go. I'm gonna go again.' I said this calmly, not screamin' at him, but calmly, matter-of-fact.

And he said, 'Well, we'll see this time, lad.'

THE COMPOUND

The mass escapes and ensuing inquiry were the inevitable results of the institutional practices that had remained free from independent scrutiny and had long been ignored by successive governments. The outcome heralded a new era in the provision of correctional treatment for young male offenders. A security unit was hurriedly opened in September. Recalcitrant inmates were confined indefinitely within this unit, and were required to participate in an extensive program of physical training in the adjacent fenced compound.

Commission of Inquiry into Abuse of Children in Queensland Institutions
Leneen Forde AC, 1999.

———————————

It was only Youngie and me, I think, who got the two years straight. The rest of them were sent back to eighteen months or otherwise dealt with and quite a few of them were released that had a much worse record than what I had, or what Youngie had. But they singled us two out. We were no more the ring-leaders than anyone else. We were all in it. It was just some spoke up a bit more than the others at the Inquiry. That was me. Youngie was picked because he was my mate.

So this happens in the afternoon and oh, the awful sick feeling in me stomach, two more years! How were we going to do two years! Holy shit, I'd just done about two years! And another two years to go!

Anyhow, the bloody black maria is out again. Out we go again, with handcuffs on us. They put us in the back and they took us back to Westbrook.

Oh, that was a terrible drive back! We're hungry, we're tired, we're sick, and we knew what we were gonna get when we got back there.

And two more years of it!

We gets back to Westbrook and are shocked to see what we see there. There's a big barbed-wire fence all along the front of the place. They open up these big gates in Westbrook, again, and they lock 'em behind us. There was a car-load of police there for when we got back.

Golledge is still there. He give me a terrible pay, Oh shit, I'm thinkin', this bloke's gonna kill me, this time, for sure. I'm terrified.

He said, 'Youse are gonna get it this time! Youse made this all happen, this is what you're gonna get.'

They marched us into this ward and then into a back ward where they'd made this security compound. They marched us through this little hallway and then into another place where we used to eat. Everything was bolted to the ground and there were big, strong lights on us. We're marched to our beds. We're given thirty seconds to get undressed and into bed, which we did in a hurry. They had that many officers around there and Golledge is waitin' for just one mistake to bash us. He didn't stop, this man.

Anyhow, this would be about nine or ten o'clock at night and we're exhausted. I was in front of the guard room where they had me right up the front. And we had to face the guard room all night. You weren't allowed to roll over. If you rolled over, they'd wake you up and make you roll over the other way again. And these bloody strong lights were in our eyes all bloody night long.

I eventually fell asleep, very late at night, and I was dead to the world in the mornin' when the bugle went. I didn't even hear it. That's very unusual for me. But I did hear something, all right. Guess who was standin' beside me, when I was still asleep. It was Golledge.

Well he was into me. Over the back of the head, punchin' into me. 'You mongrel! You snake-in-the-grass! You waster!' He was throwin' me around. I had to get dressed in a bloody hurry!

This time they'd got trained drill-masters and bloody guys from the army waitin' for us. They had different cruel men in there. Ritter, Waugh,

Moore and the rest of them, that was hand-picked for this job.

Well in this Compound, the idea was to drill ya all day long. No talkin' no smilin', nothing. It was to physically and mentally break you.

The Compound consisted of big fences of barbed wire right around. In between the Rec room and this ward. The beds were bolted to the floor, the lights were on all the time, cold showers, of course.

Well we were put out there, and we were started marchin' at five o'clock in the morning till breakfast.

'Double up, double up, run, run, run, double up, double up, run, run, run.' This went on, round and round, in circles, marchin'. All fuckin' day this went on. Five minutes break in the hour.

Our feet were achin', our shoulders were achin', oh, gracious me, this was wicked, this was unbelievable.

This went on day and night. Right till we went to bed at night they'd be drillin' us, they'd be givin' us something to do. The food was woeful what they were bringin' in to us. We were eatin' with plastic knives and forks. When they broke, they were stuck together again by lightin' a match under 'em and meltin' the plastic together again. It was just unbelievable.

This treatment was never brought out in the Forde Inquiry, it was never brought out because they'd hushed this up. They broke every law in the book in this Compound, every law in the book, they broke. Golledge wanted us smashed to bits, us lot.

And they had a set of cells made, six cells made in there. And for the slightest thing you'd do, they'd lock you up in these cells. But little did they realise, that bein' in the cells was really wonderful, you know. There was no drillin', no one screamin' in yer face.

The cells were very small, they were made of timber and there was a timber bed against the wall, with the toilet beside that. You only had a few feet to walk up and down in and there was six cells jammed up in this very small area. Ventilation was really non-existent. In summer you'd be boilin' hot and in winter, you'd be freezin'. When you were locked in there, if one of the officers didn't like yer, you probably wouldn't get any blankets till eleven o'clock at night. Some nights you got nothing whatsoever, so you'd just lay on a timber slab.

The food they dished up in there, as I said, was pathetic. I wouldn't feed my dog on it.

So it was up early in the morning and you'd start drillin' and you'd be doin' it all day long. You'd be doin' push-ups and all types of army exercises. Dolan came from the army, he was a drill-master there and Ritter, he came from Oakey, we used to call him the Oakey goat. He hadn't worked in any institutions before and neither had a lot of the rest of the officers. They'd carefully picked this select bunch of men that were sadistic. They thrived on cruelty, they loved it. They loved drillin' us, they loved the power. And we couldn't do anything about it. They had too many officers there and we just couldn't do anything about it. We copped it all day, every day.

Once a week they'd bring in a medical officer. He was a real old man who used to work in the army. So you can imagine what he was like. You'd be complainin' about something and he'd say, 'Oh, put a bit of ointment on it.' He was cold-blooded too. He was another one chosen by that crowd. This was all done by the Queensland government. Golledge did not create this situation, I'd like that to be known. The Queensland government did this, not Golledge. But Golledge was there, makin' sure that we got this treatment.

One of the officers by the name of Ryan, who came later, he was a good guy, was chosen by Sullivan when he took over, to work in the Compound after Golledge had left. This Ryan was a top man. He told me why they didn't get rid of Golledge immediately after the Schwarten Inquiry's recommendation, and have Sullivan come up from Boggo Road to take his place. They wanted to give Golledge the satisfaction of seein' us in the state we were gunna be in before he retired.

And he sure did get the satisfaction. He was down there every day. He'd say, 'Drill them parasites till they drop! You're not doin' enough to to 'em. You're not doin' enough to them wasters!'

So you can imagine, after about four months of this, we were hard as rocks. You could look in each boy's face and you could see the boy had left. And something else had creeped into his face. Something. You can't explain it. But there was no boy in us any more, he was gorn. Some of them blokes in there were fourteen or fifteen! I was sixteen.

The boy was gorn. We just looked like hardened men out of a concentration camp. There was just fear in our eyes and hate and sadness. In the end, we turned on each other. We'd fight each other, real hard, not too often but, but occasionally, we'd be into each other. Ritter was the mongrel that hated me, Waugh hated Youngie. But we eventually got the two of the bastards.

Ritter one day said I wasn't runnin' fast enough around the compound. He just didn't like me, the Oakey goat, because I was runnin' as fast as I could.

He said, 'Fletcher, do twenty body presses.'

So I done twenty and he come up to me again and says, 'Do fifty more.'

I done me fifty and then he says, 'Do two hundred.'

I couldn't move, so he kicked me.

I got up and just hooked him, just crashed him, straight in the chin. Down he went.

Waugh was on at the time. Waugh ran and pulled the siren and Golledge came roarin' down with a couple of his henchmen, Essex and Kolberg.

Kolberg didn't say nothin'. Golledge started goin' off about hookin' his men and all this crap.

I tricked old Golledge this day. I used a bit of science by now, it was no good confrontin' these people head-on, you got nowhere.

Golledge said 'I'm gonna thrash you for this, lad.'

'Sir, thrash me,' I says, 'but don't put me in the cells, Sir.'

And you know what he said? He said, 'Oh, you don't like the cells?'

So Golledge turns to his officers. 'Put him in the cells,' he says. 'Put him in the cells.' Then he give me a big lecture about 'You mob all created these cells in this place,' and he locked me in the cells.

So I got no hidin' no nothin', he just locked me in the cells.

Well, as soon as they shut the door, I was that happy! No drill, no nothin'! That done me!

So they used to keep me in the cells every night and bring me out in the daytime and drill me during the day then put me back in the cells during the night. And this went on, oh, for a long time. Plus they locked me up in the cells for about fourteen days straight. No decent showers, I wasn't taken out for a shower for seven days out of that bloody place.

Another episode from about this time concerns Youngie. He got hold of a bit of butter and he was comin' through the ward with this bit of butter in his hand and he got sprung with it by Waugh. Waugh pushed Youngie against the wall and Youngie, he hooked Waugh and give him the biggest black eye you ever seen. Youngie got put into a Bird Cage they built for us in the Compound for many months after this.

Well you could see Waugh and Ritter were just two bastards. Dolan, the trained drill master from the army, wasn't too bad. Dolan wasn't good, he was a mongrel, he drilled you all day long, screamin' at yer, but he didn't come to any violence with you. And the rest of them were the same, they just drilled you day and night. They just loved it. The power. Half of them were off the farm, the other half were brought in there specially selected by the government.

One occasion in there was very sad. I found out about this later, when I'd left the Compound.

Boonger Ryan, he was in the Compound too, with Tiers. And there was William Neilsen. They were in there a hell of a long time and they were getting' drilled to insanity, poor old Boonger and Neilson. And Boonger broke a wall down, to get out of the place. He got outside, but Neilson was trapped inside and he was being belted by the screws. So Boonger tried to get back inside, into his mate, to get him out. He takes hold of a hunk of timber and the officers are runnin' everywhere.

Well, Sullivan was runnin' Westbrook then and he could see the dangers of all this. He knew that Boonger had cracked the pot, you know, he'd gone cuckoo from this Compound. He'd gone off his rocker, and it looked like he'd turned very violent. He was just jacked up.

Well, they got the police, took the two of them away down to Ward Sixteen, which is a sort of a Loony Bin down in Brisbane and had 'em assessed.

The psychiatrist was talkin' to Boonger, askin' his questions which Boonger would have found hard to understand. So Boonger told him to 'get fucked'. Well then Boonger ends up stayin' in the rat house for nine years, you know, under pills and drugs and needles and whatnot. Nine years he did in Wacol in the Loony Bin!

Later he went to Boggo Road and he died there, young.

Now Neilson: the psychiatrist said he shouldn't even be in here, so they released him, to his surprise. He was so happy, you know, he just got released. No more Compound, nothin'. They just didn't take him back.

Who could explain the justice in this place?

But gettin' back to Ritter.

That time he kicked me in the ribs and I hooked him, well he had kicked me a few times before I hit him. He just kept on goin' and I had no out, I had to stop him. Well, anyway, there was a medical report, their own medical report that was all wrote down, about these kickin's, and I requested it from the hospital. It was woeful.

My kidneys were very badly damaged from all the jumpin' up and down and the runnin' around. The doctor had told them to lay off me on the drillin' a bit, the doctor did.

But it went on for a long time. And then eventually Golledge left and me old mate, Kevin Sullivan, a three-pipper from Boggo Road, took over Westbrook.

Him and myself were good buddies in Boggo Road. He used to write to me in Westbrook, I suppose to establish a good relationship with me for when he took over. He was a big, big man, Sullivan, and tough. He was as tall as Golledge, but a fair man. To us, anyhow.

The first thing he did when he got to Westbrook was to get down to that Compound, we'd been in there about four or five months now, maybe longer. And he cut the drillin' down by half. He said Youngie, myself and a few other guys didn't have to drill no more, we didn't have to drill. 'They can sit there and play cards or something, but they don't have to drill hard no more,' he said.

You know, the officers in there, they hated this. Here comes someone who's on the boys' side! Do you get what I'm sayin'? But, Sullivan, he knew how to run men and boys and he knew how to run officers. He knew how to treat yer. He treated us fair and there was no trouble.

And after a long period of time he made a request to the State Government, to let some blokes, includin' Youngie, out of the Compound. So they let a few of them out and I was the last one of that lot in there. They didn't let me out. Just kept me in there with half a dozen other blokes from Westbrook.

But before this happened, I'll tell you something else about what was goin' on in Westbrook. The Matron wanted a Matron's Boy. They had a Matron in there, full-time after the Inquiry, they didn't have one before, and they made Youngie the Matron's Boy.

Sullivan said, 'I want to try to let you out of here, Fletch, out of the Compound, but the government won't let you out. They want you in here. They want to make an example of you.'

That made me really dirty on that bloody government. They just had it in for me. They had to single someone out to blame for everything and I was the poor bloody turkey that they singled out.

Sullivan then approached Youngie, who had the best job in Westbrook as Matron's Boy and he said, 'Would you give up your good job to let Fletcher out of the Compound?'

Youngie said yes, so Sullivan said, 'Well, I'll make you Farm Chief.' So he was Farm Chief, which meant he could walk all round the place, around the paddocks and that.

Sullivan then came down to me and he said, 'Right, I've got you out of here. You'll work with the Matron. You'll help fix up the kids' wounds and do the barbering too.'

I'd never cut hair before in me life. I had to get out of the Compound and learn how to cut hair on the boys. But it was much better than the horse clippers, anyway, the job I did for 'em. At least their scalp was left in one piece. And bein' the Matron's boy was the best job in Westbrook.

THE RELIEVING MATRON

The most profound impact of institutional care that has flowed into adult life is the difficulty in initiating and maintaining stable, loving relationships. Without a nurturing environment, with too few, or no, adults to give love and affection, many care leavers were unable to develop the skills needed to build mature adult relationships once they had left the institution behind.

Forgotten Australians:
Senate Committee Report on Australians who experienced institutional
or out-of-home care as children. 2004

Now I'm goin' to tell you a story about when Santa Claus came to Westbrook. Now this Santa didn't have no long white beard and red suit and give out presents to everyone. This Santa had short dark hair and soft white skin and took over while the other matron was away for a while. This Santa Claus was the relievin' matron.

She was a good looker, probably about thirty years of age, well to me she looked about thirty. Probably could have been forty or fifty, I don't know.

She got me to get permission to go down to the house where she was livin' which was quite a distance from the back of the dairy, and out-of-bounds to me because I was supposed to stay around the front of the office at all times, where they could keep an eye on me. I was watched twenty-four hours a day, bein' an escapee.

This day she requested that I come down and help her move furniture.

I had no say in the matter. Naturally, I was quite happy to be goin' down and movin' furniture for her, gettin' out of the place for a while. So I asked Superintendent Sullivan and he said, 'By all means, go down there.'

So I go down there this day and when I arrive there I knocked on the back door.

She said, 'Come in, Al.'

So I push open the door and close it behind me and there's the relievin' matron, skippin' out of the shower with just a towel around her.

Well, you know, I sort of turn my head the other way, naturally, but I couldn't help havin' a little peep.

She came up to me and she said, 'You must be feelin' a bit hot, here.'

I was scared. I didn't know what was goin' on here, because, not havin' had sex.

(Well actually, I did have sex once in Newstead Park, but I was only fourteen at the time and it was a quickie. But this was completely different.)

Well she kissed me and played with me and then took my hand and we went into the bedroom. She laid down on the bed, she'd dropped the towel by this time of course and we had quite a good romp. For about three hours. She was my teacher, I suppose, she taught me how to enjoy sex.

The next day she had cigarettes for me. She didn't smoke herself, but she went and got me some cigarettes for afterwards, and we had a cup of tea and cake.

And this went on for seven days. It was like Santa Claus came to Westbrook, for Crow Fletcher. Yes, Santa Claus came and stayed at Westbrook for about seven days. I'd be down there every day movin' furniture. Until at the end, it started to look a bit smelly. And people were thinkin'.

The Superintendent says to me, 'Still moving furniture, Crow! She must have a lot of furniture down there!'

And I said, 'Oh you know, Sir. She doesn't really know what she wants. She wants it here and then she wants it there. '

It ended as abruptly as it had started.

But I must admit, she sure taught me how to enjoy sex. She left after a few weeks and the other Matron came back. And of course, she wouldn't have a bar of that type of thing.

I suppose this episode would have had some bearin' on me not wantin' to stay any longer in that place. I thought, Holy Mackerel, what am I missin' out on here? I'm outa here. I'll get to that Sydney again and I'll romp like hell!

Of course, you have to understand that I kept this very quiet. I did tell Youngie, me mate, about it, because we was very close. And he was the Matron's Boy before me, as you've already read.

Youngie was not very happy about it at all. He said, 'Here I am, I give up my job for you, and Santa Claus comes to you for a whole week. What about me?'

I said, 'Well look, Youngie, mate, Al got in first. Santa came to the Crow, and Youngie, you missed out.'

He said, 'Is there any way that you can make out you're real sick and I could come back and take over your job for a week. Or two?'

'It'd be impossible, mate. How could we work it?'

So we thought about it, but nothing eventuated. Not that I thought anything would eventuate. But you can see the funny side of this.

AS THE CROW FLIES

Golledge was replaced by Kevin Sullivan, a former prison warder. New regulations were introduced which set guidelines for the use of corporal punishment, a privilege system was instituted to facilitate better classification of inmates according to their behaviour, and a major rebuilding program was undertaken.

Many more offenders were now being sentenced to detention, most of whom came from the Brisbane metropolitan area. There was also evidence to indicate that the recidivism rate was increasing and that greater numbers of indigenous youths were being admitted.

Commission of Inquiry into Abuse of Children in Queensland Institutions
Leneen Forde AC, 1999.

With Sullivan, Westbrook improved in lots of ways. The food improved, the clothing situation improved. Out of the Inquiry came gigantic improvements on the time Golledge was there. Sullivan even said he was trying to get special permission to get us out of that two–year period of straight sentence. But to do that, you'd have to take it through the courts and all. The most you could get off was three weeks.

Youngie and me, we got talking about it all and we said 'We're gunna be here for this full two years. There's no way Sullivan can get us out. We'll go, we'll end up goin' again.' We knew that in our minds.

But what really put the icing on the cake was all those other boys who were with us in the breakout from Westbrook got released, bar about two of them, but even they were goin' to get out shortly in a few months, anyhow. So we were there now for another twelve months or longer and we said, What's the good of stayin' here? We have to do another twelve months. Sullivan can't get us out. We're here, but all the rest of them, they've gorn home.' They released the rest of those boys, but not Youngie and me.

So we were in Top Ward, that was a very small, privileged section of Westbrook where you had good clothes and a TV set to watch at night. There were maybe ten or fifteen boys at most, in there.

There were three sections, the main section was just the ordinary boys and you had to be real good to get up to Top Ward, you know. Then there was the Compound when you misbehaved, and it didn't take much to put you into the Compound. Didn't take much at all.

The officers treated us okay when we got put into the good jobs because they didn't want no more trouble and while Sullivan was runnin' the place there was definitely a different atmosphere there.

They made us sergeants. That means we had to make sure the other boys wouldn't run away. So we were in the open, actually. Every Saturday night, for three or four minutes, the boys would be marched up and we'd stand on the outside of them with the screws and officers in the different sections. This was when we would be marchin' the boys, everybody, except the boys in the Compound, up to the Rec room for the movies. And this Saturday night, Youngie said to me, 'We'll go tonight.'

We made up our minds suddenly, that night, because Sullivan wasn't on. 'We'll go from here.'

So someone yells out 'Sergeants fall out!', that's Youngie and me. We wouldn't touch any of the kids or hook 'em or anything. It was a different era, as I said, with Sullivan in charge. But we'd stop 'em if they ran. That's what they thought, anyway.

So they're all marchin' up to Top Wards and Youngie and me were up the front and Youngie sings out, 'Let's go!' and we bolted. The Sergeants bolted. We bolted out of the bloody place.

We'd waited until, I think, Essex was on. We didn't like him, but we liked Sullivan, so we didn't want to bolt on that man. Well anyhow, we bolted from there and we got into Toowoomba and we pinched a car, an

FJ Holden. Nobody chased us, by the way, they just let us go.

We drove the Holden down to Brisbane and dumped the car. I got to my mother's place, where I slept under the bed all night. Youngie was supposed to meet me the next day, but he got caught.

It was on the TV about us, but nothin' too bad. It just said that there were two Westbrook escapees and they had our names and our photos.

My mother couldn't understand me sleepin' under her bed. I couldn't explain the fear that was in me, to her. I don't know what she made of me, she just couldn't understand all this. She could have got into a lot of trouble harbourin' me too. And my stepfather Abe, he was good enough to put up with this as well. He was a very nervous man, poor old Abe, and here's me, over the TV and all. His whole family was well-to-do people and very honest. But he was a good man, he never commented, that bloke, never commented.

So anyhow, me Nanna got some money together and they worked it out. They got me on a flight to Sydney. They disguised me, put a hat on me, made me look like a jockey, actually. And I went under the name of Lester, on the plane ticket. So Mr Lester then left Brisbane on a big Boeing—straight through to Sydney.

SYDNEY

Children placed under the guardianship—custody, care and control—of the state... had as their legal guardian the Minister, Director or other official of a state welfare department.
In general, the guardian of the child was granted extensive authority to make major decisions for the child.

Forgotten Australians:
Senate Committee Report on Australians who experienced institutional
or out-of-home care as children. 2004

Well I get into Sydney and I have nowhere to go so I head for Robin Parnell's place. Robin Parnell was the bloke who escaped early in my time at Westbrook, he only done three months there. He was also the one who done the paintings for me to give to the Forde Inquiry. Robin just stayed in Sydney, workin' and they never bothered him, because in them days, they couldn't extradite you to Queensland.

It was a funny set-up, old Frank Dowling, he'd broken out of Westbrook too, and he's down in Sydney. Graham, he'd broken out too and he was in Sydney. Kenny Johnson and Bushnell, they'd broken out and they were livin' in Sydney. So there was a small gang of us escapees all livin' in the same suburb. Some were workin', some weren't, some were just layin' around the house, because they didn't care about anything, no more.

Well I had ambitions, then. I felt very sorry that Youngie had gone back in there. I knew what he must have been goin' through the year that I was away. And I got a job in Sieber's bakehouse wrapping Dr

Vogel's bread. I did very well there. I learned how to work this first big wrappin' machine they ever had and I could have worked anywhere in Australia with it, because I had the knowledge of it. And I never went out at night, or anything. I used to go to work early in the mornin' and just stay home when I knocked off.

I met a lovely girl, Lynette Aurisch and we were thinkin' of gettin' engaged and one day, gettin' married. But unfortunately, her German, so-called well-to-do people, found out all about this whole Westbrook episode and they made sure the marriage didn't eventuate. To this day I've missed her as a person and I believe it's the same with her, but that's the way it goes. You never get what you want in this world.

Anyhow, for about nine months or whatever it was down there, I kept every pay slip, I had 'em all in a big bundle, and with Graham, who was workin' in Sydney too, we decided we'd go back and see our folk in Brisbane. And we went back to Brisbane and Graham and me were thinkin' gee it'd be good to go back home again, live up here and get a job and not be on the run in Sydney, all the time.

Well, we decided to go in and give it a try in the State Children's Department. We'd prove to them that we got jobs and prove to them that we did the right thing. We'd see if they would release us.

We went in there early one morning and asked for the man in charge, whoever he was. And we spoke to this head guy in the State Children's Department. We said who we were and I proved to them all the work that I'd done. I showed them all my pay slips and told them that I had a job here in Brisbane to go to, and Graham had a job here in Brisbane to go to, and now we'd like to be set free.

They said they would set us free. They said what a wonderful job we'd both done, you know, how we'd got work, and especially me. They said 'What a wonderful job you've done with yourself.'

They rang up my mother and they told her, 'How'd you like to have your son home for good, now? We're going to set him free.' And they did the same thing to Graham's mother, they said the same thing to her. So they officially released us.

Now, this is the big one. We're as happy as Larry, we're free. At last.

But not for long. This bloke says, 'Ahh, come in on Wednesday, next week and you can sign the release papers.' He says 'I've just got to get them officially signed by Mr Clarke. We have to wait until he comes back, he's up north and he said he'll be back for when you come in to sign the papers.'

Now Mr Clarke was voted The Father of the Year and we go in this morning to sign the papers, thinkin' everything was normal. In them days you could have a smoke in the buildings, no one minded, and we were just sittin' down on the couch there, havin' a smoke, happy as anything, and the next thing this Clarke walks out. 'Put those cigarettes out,' he says. 'Put 'em out, you pair.'

And I said, 'Well other people are smokin' here, Sir.' I'm thinkin' something's up here, but I wasn't too sure.

He tells us to come into his office and we go in there and we're respectably dressed and we're standin' there, properly, respectfully, and he says, 'You're going back to Westbrook.'

I said, 'We came in here to sign our release papers.'

He said, ' No, you're going back to Westbrook.'

I said 'I'm not goin' back to Westbrook. You'd have to carry me back to Westbrook.' I thought he was jokin'.

He wasn't jokin'.

Next minute, some coppers came out of the back room, about four of them. This was all a big set-up. They could have got us the first time. They didn't have to set us up like this to do their dirty work.

Westward was one of the people workin' for the State Government then and I told him, 'I'm not goin' back. You're goin' to have to carry me back there. And if you do put me back there,' I said, 'I'm gonna wreck your place and I'm gonna go again. I'm gonna wreck it this time. I'm gonna really cause some trouble. I'm seventeen years of age, I'd rather be in gaol. I'd rather be in Boggo Road Gaol.'

Graham was a very solid man, you know, as a mate. He was a tall guy, Graham and he was a very solid friend. They said to Graham, 'Look, you go back now, without any trouble and you'll be out in no time.'

I wish now, that Graham had left me, for what he had to go through, what he had to endure by being a staunch friend.

But anyhow, that was not my fault, really, but I did wish later that he'd left me then, for his own sake. I think I did say, 'Go, you go with him, Graham.' And he said, 'No, I'm not goin' with him. I'm standin' by you.'

And he told Clarke straight, he said, 'I'm stickin' by Fletcher, I'm stickin' by Crow. Wherever he goes, I'm stickin' by him.'

The coppers said, 'Well come on, off we go,' and I sat on the floor. Graham didn't, but I just sat on the floor.

I said, 'No, you carry me out of here. Carry me out of here and you can show everybody what you people are doin'.

Oh, he was dirty, this Clarke. The coppers didn't say much. They just got hold of me, one on each arm and leg and they carried me through the hallway. People are lookin'. Then we're out on the street and up to the cop car and people everywhere are just lookin'. Graham's just walkin' along normal, with only one officer holdin' onto his arm.

These two carryin' me out put me in the police car. Then the sergeant leant over the back seat and he said, 'Here have a good cigarette'. We only had tobacco—'have a good one.' He said, 'Look, this is woeful! I can see you are in your rights for what's gone on here. We are only the police, we get told what to do. We can't do anything more than this ... And look,' he said—I think he called me Al, 'Look Al, you'll walk into the watch-house now and make it easy for us, won't you?'

I said, 'Yair, I've got no argument with you guys, you're just doin' your job, but you can see what they done there. You just tell everybody what they did in this bloody place to us today. They broke our bloody hearts! And now we've got to go back again and there's about nine more bloody months in that place.' I said, 'I can't do it, I've had a taste of freedom, a taste of happiness in my life. And now I'm back there again.'

And Graham just groaned, put his hand to his head, and said, 'Fuck, what am I into here?'

Anyhow they put us in the watch-house. The sergeant was real good in there. He said, 'Let 'em have smokes in the cell up there because this is a joke!' He said to a lot of the officers in the Brisbane watch-house. 'This is a joke! This whole thing's a joke!'

They put two officers with us to drive us back to Westbrook. Up around Gatton somewhere, they pulled up to buy some vegetables from a stall on the side of the road.

But before they stopped, the sergeant said to the other officer, 'Look why don't we just turn our back and let 'em bolt? Turn our backs! Let 'em go!'

But the young bloke, he said, 'It's all right for you, you're retirin' in two weeks. I've got the rest of me life in the Police Force. I'd be in it, you know, but I've got a wife and kids to feed.'

The sergeant said, 'Oh, let 'em go. Just turn our backs and let 'em go.'

They didn't. They just bought some fruit and vegies and that. Then they pulled up again and bought a packet of fags. The sergeant said, 'Here, you better get a few of these inter yer before you get there.' You know, he really was a kind old bloke.

Anyhow, back through the gates of Westbrook. Here I am back.

Poor old Youngie, he's in the Compound. They've got him locked in a little old bird cage they built for him. They had him in there for three or four months because they could not control him no more. He was uncontrollable. Youngie had just jacked up on 'em and that was that. So they locked him in the cells every night, and brought him into the Compound every day. He refused to drill any more. We were gettin' big boys by now. They were handlin' all the little boys that had just come in and they had them pretty well trained. 'Yes Sir, no Sir, three bags full.' But we were too tough. We were too hardened up by now and they knew it. No more boys in us, we were men. Hard men. Hard men from sixteen onwards, after the Boggo Road episode.

Well the sergeant handed us over to one of the officers and straight into the Compound we go. Youngie was glad to see me back as he had a little plan goin' there for some time but needed somebody that was solid enough to go with him, game enough to escape from this place.

Graham was there beside me. We were treated okay. No belt, no nothin'. Sullivan came down and said to me, 'Look. I'm gonna go out of my way to get you out of here. Don't do anything wrong. Don't do anything wrong. You don't have to drill. Just lay on the beds in here durin' the day and play cards.'

All the officers in there treated me real good. I'm not goin' to say there was anything wrong, the last time I went back there. They all kept comin' up to me durin' the day and they'd say, 'Now don't do nothin'. You're goin' to get out of here. We're goin' to get you out of here in. ' some said six weeks, some said three weeks.

But in my own heart I knew, or thought I knew, that there was no way Andrews was goin' to break that two-year sentence. Look at all the times I'd been before him and escaped.

They really believed that they were goin' to get me out, though.

Youngie wasn't gettin' out apparently because he attacked Waugh, givin' him a terrible black eye.

Now while Graham and me were there, there was that good officer by the name of Ryan there who was put on by Sullivan. He was turnin' out to be a good mate, Ryan was. Even later in life, Ryan used to come to my home and sleep overnight. He was a good officer. He'd give us cigarettes and that and we'd have cigarettes during the day. Not openly, naturally. But it was known that we were smokin' up there, which was unheard of, but they put up with it.

The Matron came down there every day and she'd talk to me and she'd say, 'Don't do anything wrong, they're really fighting to get you out of here. It's wrong what's gone on here, the whole thing, we want you out. You and Graham, we're going to get you out.'

But Youngie said, 'No matter what they do, they can't get you out of here. It's got to go before the District Court and Andrews has got to okay it.

Anyhow I owed him a favour, the poor bastard, he done all that time in there when I was in Sydney and as I say again, I had no qualms about any of the officers and how I was treated when I went back there. But deep in my heart, I felt betrayed and hurt, and so did Graham. To be released and free and then be told to come in to sign the release papers and be put back in this.

So I said to Youngie, 'Okay, I'll go with you.' But I added, 'If this plan doesn't work, we're goin' to barricade ourselves in here and we won't let 'em in under any circumstances. We've got to go to gaol, because they'll fuckin' murder us in here if we upset 'em again! They'll kill us! And I can't do nine months in this bloody place, or six months, or whatever it is, I can't do it and I don't intend to do it. Now you know where I stand. I'm not lettin' any officers into this security section, I'm goin' to barricade it up. If things go wrong, I'm gonna wait until the reporters come here and I'd rather die in here, than go outside and be caught again.'

So he knew where I stood. I said to Graham, 'Are you with us or are you goin' to stay, Graham?' and he said, 'No, I'm goin' with youse.' So this night, this was the plan.

Over the last six months that Youngie was in the Compound he was bouncin' a medicine ball off one of the walls there. Six months solid. He said 'I've weakened this wall, this wall will fall down.'

I said, 'Oh, yair. I hope so.'

So the plan was that Youngie walks over to the wall and pulls the end of the boards down until there's a gap we can get through. I guard the doors.

We did it on the mongrels, Ritter, Waugh, and Dolan, that big-mouthed army drill-master. We made sure that Sullivan wasn't on again, 'cause he was all right. With me he was okay. With him there the place was a hundred percent better than it was before. And where they used to have a hundred and thirty boys, they only had about fifty in this Home by now. So the place was a lot better, a lot easier for everybody.

So Youngie goes over to the wall, there, and I light up a cigarette in front of the officers and blow the smoke at them. They were in shock. And I will admit it, I urinated on the floor in front of them and lit up another cigarette. They hadn't moved, they were just in shock.

They were sort of locked into another section, there. They had another guard that used to come and unlock that section. And they went for the siren immediately, 'cause they could see something was definitely wrong. And of course we'd plugged the siren, so it wouldn't work

Youngie pulled the board from the outside and I rushed over and helped him for a second, then I got back to the door and held the door with me foot against the bed, so they couldn't get in, which they didn't even try, they were just shittin' themselves.

We kicked the outside boards off, and then we all piled out.

About three-quarters of the kids in the security compound climbed through this gap in the wall.

Then we had to climb over a very tall barbed-wire fence, through the Compound, over another fence and then on top of the Big Rec room. I done a little dance on top of the Rec room, tellin' them all what I thought of them and what the government had done to us. Then we slid down and we bolted through the back of the Orchard.

Graham went through but he went the wrong way. He went the back way where there was plenty more barbed-wire fences to get over. He got caught in there. A few of the other boys got hung up by their arms in the barbed wire, too, they were just hangin' there and one guy nearly lost his thumb through it all, I find out about all this later.

Youngie and me, we're boltin' and we're on our way to Toowoomba. No one's chasin' us and a young bloke by the name of Murdoch is with us. You've probably read a lot about him in the newspapers and the tremendous crimes that he committed, terrible crimes. He was only very young, about fourteen, I think, when he was with us.

And we think, Ah shit. We've got a young kid with us and this'll bring us undone.

Anyhow, we gets into Toowoomba, which is about an eighteen-mile bloody walk, all we had on us was a pair of pyjamas. We had no shoes and no belt, so we're bare-footed all the way in to there and we gets to the Toowoomba Hospital where we we've gotta get some clothes. So we walk around the side there and we seen a window open and there was some clothes there, so I hopped through the window and grabbed some and passed them out to Youngie. I also went into the fridge and got some food.

One of the nurses came in and she sprung me. She said 'What are you doin' robbin' the fridge for?'

I just jumped straight through the window and we bolted, with all the food, a pillowcase full of food and all these clothes, hospital gowns. So we got further away from the hospital, a coupla hundred yards, and we changed our clothes and had something to eat. Then we said,

'Murdoch, you stay here and we'll go and try to get a car. That's the only way we'll get out of here.'

So we're dressed up in these funny white gowns and we went for one car and someone came out and we bolted. I don't know what they thought they seen that night, runnin' down the road and over fences with these big white gowns on, but we eventually got a car, an FJ Holden. You could kick them over with a bit of silver paper, they were very easy to steal.

We couldn't get back to Murdoch, it was impossible. We seen a police car further up and we wouldn't take the chance of goin' back.

Graham was caught, all the rest of them were caught, but we proceeded through to Brisbane. We drove out Grovely way and we dumped the car round Enoggera. I went to me father's place where I hid out for maybe three or four days. Our escape was on the news, it was quite a big deal. My father's next door neighbour knew we were there, Jack McBride, a good man. He never said nothing.

Then the same old story. We got disguised by Nanna and she bought our plane tickets to Sydney. I still used my old name, Lester. Youngie used the name of Fisher. We boarded a plane then and went to Sydney and we lived at Glebe, just off Glebe Point Road. We stayed there and worked and we did not come back to Brisbane until the two years was up.

This law has since changed. Now if you have not completed your sentence and have escaped, you go back and finish it off.

BACK IN BRISBANE

Governments and the public are rightly intensely concerned about the potential mayhem of terror on public transport and in public places in Australia, resulting in hundreds of deaths and injuries. They are rightly trying as hard as possible to address the problem.

They should also be concerned at the terror experienced by our children.

A reign of terror occurred in too many child-care institutions, resulting in thousands of suicides, many tens of thousands of sexual assaults, hundreds of thousands of physical assaults, and consequent trauma for many of the adults those children became.

Research shows that a disproportionate percentage of the prison population are care leavers, or those who have suffered abuse and assaults as children.

Growing up in 'care' in twentieth-century Australia
Senator Andrew Murray, September 2005

When the two years was up, we came back to Brisbane and we were free.

I rang up Superintendent Sullivan and said I wanted my money that I earned in that place and I wanted my tobacco. And I went down to the government department and they gave me some measly amount of money. They owed me a hell of a lot more, for instance the money that Nanna had put in trust for me, but I never ever did get that. I did receive something later but I knocked back the pathetic amount that they offered me then. I also got the couple of packets of tobacco which was from Boggo Road that had been sent to us, but not given to us. And I went back up the road and rang Sullivan up and Sullivan was real good. He said. 'I'm glad you're finally free and I'm glad you never came back here and I'm glad you didn't end up in gaol.'

I said, 'I don't intend to end up in gaol.'

He said, 'You go back down to that department there. How long would it take to walk down there?'

I said, 'About ten minutes.'

He said, 'Well I'll be in contact with them by the time you get there and they'll have something for you, don't you worry about that.'

Youngie didn't think we'd pull this off, but he teamed along.

Anyhow they gave us all the tobacco. All the tobacco for all the boys that were in Boggo Road gaol, they gave to us. And they gave me something like thirty or forty dollars. They also give Youngie ten or twenty dollars. That was from all the vegetables we sold from there. I asked them about all the money my Nanna had put in for me. They said they'd go all through that and get back to me on the matter. Well, I didn't keep the matter goin'. I was quite happy just to get what we got, bein' broke as we were, and we went across the road and went to the pub and celebrated our final release from Westbrook.

After this apparently there were other enquiries into Westbrook.

But after Sullivan left, the place went back into its old routine. It was always in the news, there was always trouble there and in the end, you know, the Beattie government took over and Anne Warner wrote me a very nice letter sayin' they were goin' to close Westbrook down for good. In the letter she said something like 'This should make you happy now, we're closin' it down for good and hopefully, you can get on with your life.'

Well that's about the end of the story, except what happened to Graham after they caught him from that escape, was pretty shockin'.

His mother used to be in contact with my mother. She told her they drilled him and drilled him until he was skin and bone and looked like he come out of a Concentration camp. What they did to that poor boy! What he must have went through I can just imagine, all because we pulled that wall down! He did about twelve more months in there and his mother told us what was happenin' to him and oh, it was frightenin'!

I dunno what would have happened to us. Thank goodness we never went back. We were finally freed from that hell.

Murdoch they did the same to. Murdoch went on to be a very bad criminal and some of the other guys that went out through that wall that night, they got into a lot of trouble in their lives too, always in newspapers for vicious crimes and such.

Another point I must bring up. We're free now. And about a year later, I decided to go back down and live in Sydney. I was driving around without a licence, no one cared, but I went up to the local cop shop at Michelton Police. And I decided to get a learner's permit. So I went in to get a learner's permit and one of the officers said, 'Yeah, yeah, you're right, mate.'

But Big Jim at Mitchelton, he didn't like me, this mongrel. He said, 'No, hold on to him, we want to charge him. He's got a couple of outstanding warrants.'

I'm thinking, Ahh, shit, it's on again.

They didn't know who Youngie was, he was in this too, so I called him some other name and I said 'Could you go and get me some tobacco, it looks like I'm goin' to gaol again.'

I said, 'Just take the car and go. Get out of here.'

So he went down and got me some tobacco and he took the car and went.

The other coppers said to Big Jim, 'Let him go, let him go, it's all to do with this bloody Westbrook, it's ridiculous. The whole thing's ridiculous!'

Big Jim says, 'No, no. I've rang up Detective Keats and Bacchi and they're comin' out now to arrest him.'

So the detectives come out and they're real good. They arrested me for breakin' and enterin' at the hospital, I only hopped through a window, but 'breakin' and enterin' and 'illegal use of a motor vehicle'.

They took me down to my grandmother's place and they said, 'Can you rake up a hundred pound bail? We're putting the lowest one we can on him. You need to get him out of there straight away if you can.'

She said, 'Yeah, I can get the money.' Nanna always came good. She couldn't have been a better mother to me and my sister than a real mother, when we was children.

'Well, get him out of that watch-house,' says the detective.

So this all happens and some months later I have to go before the court. And you can guess who it was I have to appear before. Old Judge Dormer George Andrews again.

But he pulled out of the case.

He handed over to a bloke by the name of Wansell. See, he couldn't try this case after I'd not done his two years and busted the whole place down. And not only that, the government had got to him and said, 'Give him the lot. Throw the book at him.' This was my pay-back, see. They planned it. They had a plan for me, to get even on me for escapin' Westbrook, and for the Inquiry, and the whole lot.

Well, thanks to the goodness of Andrews, he spoke to Wansell and he fined me on all accounts. They fined me for this and they fined me for that, and I was already on probation for two years. Flynn was the Probation officer and I would have to go in to see him at the Old Mansions in George Street. But it was done that way that I never went to gaol, even though I broke my probation.

After the case, Keats and Bacchi said , 'Come on Al. Come down the pub. We're goin' to buy you a beer.' They treated me good, too. They said it never should have ever come into the court, but what could they do? They had their job to do.

Next time I saw Flynn he told me that Judge Andrews wanted to see me in his chambers.

So I went along and after this I became very good friends with the Judge. I used to often go up to his chambers in the new Supreme Court building and have a cup of coffee with him and a cigarette. He used to smoke Country Life, once. I always remember that. He didn't smoke later on in his life, and he only had one arm, you know, he lost one arm during the war when he was a fighter pilot. They used to call him the 'one-armed bandit' on account of it.

And when I had no money, or anything, I often used to drop in there and bite him for a few bob and he always helped me out. He gave me very good advice and told me quite a few things. Once he said to me, 'Don't you ever come before me, whatever happens, don't ever come before me again. I've only got one arm, and I don't want to lose this one I've got left.'

He told me that there was people in the government that were still out to get me for all the trouble I caused them. So that was why I was never ever to come before him again. Him gettin' Wansell to take my case that last time, was to let me off the hook. I think he really stuck his neck out for me, then.

He also said, 'When your term of probation ends, I strongly advise you to leave Brisbane for a while.'

So I took his advice and went to Sydney, among other places, for a few years.

When I got back to Brisbane, we kept in touch. We even sent each other Christmas cards.

Once I called into his chambers and I'd been drinkin' and I was feelin' a bit crook. Andrews says to me, 'Just lie down on the couch there for a while, until you feel a bit better. I'll let security know you are in here and when you want to go, they'll let you out of the building.'

So I had a lay down on the couch with a cushion under me head and fell asleep. And when I woke up, he'd gone home, it was around eight o'clock at night. Anyhow, I gets up and walks out of his rooms and the security guard is there and he lets me out of the building, no trouble at all.

He tried nine hundred odd cases apparently, in the District Court in Brisbane. And I said to him once, 'What case stands out in your mind the most?'

He paused a moment and a smile flickered over his face. Then he said, 'Well, your case.'

Recently I heard he was a very ill man and livin' somewhere down the coast. He'd invited me to come and see him and bring me wife and boy down with me. I hadn't seen him for a few years and fully intended goin' down to see him again and I mentioned this to another bloke who knew him. And he says, 'Old Dormer? He died just last week.'

So I missed out on seein' him one last time before he died. He died while this book was bein' written.

For some reason he took an interest in me. I heard that he'd give people a go if he thought they had a tough upbringin', but that he'd throw the book at you if he thought you were a violent criminal or had a reasonable go in life and no excuses for your behaviour.

Life is very strange. What odds would you give a 'Brook boy bein' friends with the judge that tried him? Yet we became mates. And now he's gone, it makes me sad to think I won't be seein' him no more.

Anyway, that's me story, I've told it and no one can call me a liar because I've got the evidence to prove all I've said. When you've been institutionalised it's hard to settle down to what might be called a normal life. You see things different. But I guess I might be one of the lucky ones who got out of Westbrook and lived to tell the tale. A lot of the boys that was in there with me are dead. In later years they suicided or the grog got 'em, same thing I suppose.

Now that I've told me tale I might give the 'Brook a rest. Or, more to the point, it might give me a rest. It don't exist no more as a 'Farm Home ' or a juvenile detention centre. I have that letter from Anne Warner and Peter Beattie to say they closed it in 1999. Same year as the Forde Inquiry. What a coincidence. They've closed Boggo Road Gaol, too and they've lost all the records about the fifteen of us Westbrook boys bein' put in there after the Schwarten Inquiry. They say the floods destroyed 'em. All I can say is a lot of people in high places must be very grateful to them floods. They supposedly destroyed a lot of our history. But I've collected a few records which weren't destroyed by the floods and I've got 'em here for your perusal, plus a lot more besides. You might find 'em interestin' readin'.

© AL FLETCHER
(The Crow) 2004

Excerpts from the Schwarten Inquiry:

Westbrook Farm Home for Boys
Mr AE Schwarten, Stipendary Magistrate
27th September 1961

*(Editor's note: Most of the spellings, grammar and punctuation used in the report
are reproduced here. Where misspellings etc. confuse meaning however, they have
been corrected. Boys' reference numbers have been removed for security reasons and
page references removed to facilitate ease of reading.*
*Although only about 30 pages of the report were released to the public, references in
those page indicate that the report ran to at least 2000 pages.)*

Amount of corporal punishment not declared to inmate.

I can think of nothing more degrading, more destructive to human dignity and
pride than these public beltings, which until recently were with the inmates'
trousers down. That this should have been permitted to have been done to any boy,
particularly boys of 16 years and 17 years, seems incredible. Such things, not only
scar and callous the body, but they also callous and scar the mind. The only result
would be to build hatred and resentment, not only in the inmates so punished, but
also in those compelled to see and hear, or rather to hear only as the inmates say
that it was the unwritten law that on such occasions the inmates turn their heads
away and refuse to see. In this the inmates demonstrated finer instincts and greater
human understanding than the administration. These public strappings must also
have seriously militated against the Home's intended purpose of rehabilitation and
reformation. Public strappings should be immediately abandoned.

It appears that when an inmate was to be strapped for some breach, the number
of strikes he is to receive is not declared and made known to him. Some of the
inmates say that the Superintendent carries on until the inmate caves in and says

'Oh sir' or 'Oo sir'.

The Superintendent whilst admitting that he does not inform the inmate the number of strikes he is to receive, denies this. He says 'I do not give them more punishment because they would not show it was hurting. I have a set idea that I will give him so many. say eight. He may be a fellow you will hit a couple of times and he does break down to a point. and you let him go, but also you get some fellows who say in the yard 'He will not make me sing out'. If that fellow comes up he may get a few extra and that is all there is to it.' This does not sound to me like one in authority exercising due discretion impartially and properly and determining the amount of punishment according to the circumstances and nature of the particular breach. Until Regulations are framed laying down the maximum number of strikes that may be inflicted for particular breaches, the Superintendent would be well-advised to determine the number of strikes according to the nature and circumstances of the particular breach and declare the number to the inmate before administering the corporal punishment.

Form of address to inmates.

Complaints were made by the inmates that they were spoken to in insulting terms by the Superintendent and certain warders. Inmates claim that the Superintendent used expressions towards them such as 'guttersnipe', 'parasite'. 'waster', 'blackdog', 'black mongrel' and on occasions would refer to an inmate's parents in derogatory terms .

The Superintendent denies all these allegations stating that such terms were only used by him to describe to an inmate the type of breach he had been guilty of, such as 'real mongrel action' or 'real waster type of thing to do'.

A perusal of the punishment book reveals that in describing the inmates in the punishment book the Superintendent has on occasions inserted such expressions as: 'perfect waster', 'no hoper', 'darkies', 'poor type of darky', 'bad poor type of aboriginal', 'Frightful type', 'poorest type possible to find', 'low bad type that will know nothing but jail life', 'aboriginal of poor quality', 'typical nigger'.

An inmate who was crying ...dismissed with a facetious remark 'I'll get a titty bottle for you to suck on lad'.

Coloured inmates.

Claims by the inmates that there was discrimination by the Superintendent against the colored inmates were fairly frequent. In effect, the inmates state that the colored inmates receive a greater number of strikes which were inflicted with greater force than would be applied to a white inmate guilty of a similar breach of the rules .

'While he was belting the dark lads, he (Superintendent Golledge) called them black wasters and parasites. He really wales into them. You can tell he does not like them.'

This is a most serious accusation to bring against a person in authority who is called upon to administer impartial justice, as the Superintendent is, and if proved would demonstrate that persons unfitness for his position.

Castor Oil.

'Shades of Mussolini'. The Superintendent claimed that castor oil was administered not as a punishment but as a health precaution . I do not believe this. The castor oil was administered in such circumstances and in such a way that it could only be a punishment. Castor oil as an aperient was abandoned at least 25 years ago. Further, the punishment book of 10th December, 1957, contains the following entry: Boy ? Eating green beans in yard knowing this is prohibited.'

The punishment recorded in the book is 'dose of castor oil' and the Entry is initialed 'I.R.G.' which are the initials of the Superintendent.

This is the only castor oil punishment recorded in the punishment book although Reg. 107 requires the recording of all complaints and all punishments.

The Superintendent claimed that the dose administered was two tablespoon-fuls, the inmates say it was nearer one half bottle. From the manner in which the oil was administered I would say that the inmates were nearer the mark for from the methods used the Superintendent could have little control and little idea of the quantity partaken. The Superintendent admits that the oil was administered by holding back the head of the inmate and pouring the oil direct from the bottle into the open mouth and down the throat of the inmate. In the process, from instinctive revulsion some of the oil would spill on the inmate's clothes and he would be compelled to wear those clothes until the following Sunday, change day. The following are instances of castor oil punishment: Boy ? eating raw cabbage from his own garden bed, Boy ? for eating stolen cauliflower, Boy ? for wetting pants, Boy ?

for eating green beans and one pea, Boy ? for eating beans, Boys ?and ? for eating stolen grapes. Both deny that they actually ate any grapes.

Boys ? and ? were also strapped the punishment book at showing Boy ? ten cuts and Boy ? eight cuts. Both Boys ? and ?claimed that they received 15 cuts. Boy ? for eating carrots from own garden bed, Boys ? and ? for having one peach in their possession. These two youths also claimed that they received 9 or 10 cuts with the strap. The punishment book contains no record of this corporal punishment. Except for boys ? and ? all the above recipients were schoolboys.

In my opinion the punishment was revolting in itself and in its method and the purging it must have caused could have been harmful.

Walking the path.

This was a punishment imposed mainly by the warders for minor breaches of discipline such as talking on parade and apparently when an inmate was put on the path he was not informed nor any decision made as to the duration of the period but he would be taken off the path when it was later considered that he had been there a sufficient time. It was also always imposed by the Superintendent as an additional punishment to the strapping of absconders and attempted absconders. From the evidence I gathered the impression that this type of punishment was frequently imposed.

When the punishment was imposed it was not entered in the punishment book as required by Reg.107.

The 'path' is a stretch of ground approximately 25-30 yards in length and the inmate was required to walk up and down this distance at a brisk pace.

He had to walk this path every spare moment of his time. That is, he would be walking this path every minute of his waking time, except for time taken for meals, ablution, toilet and time spent working with his allotted working party. In the evening he was not allowed to join in recreation but had to stand out at attention in the recreation room. The rule of silence was also imposed upon inmates walking the path. The only spare time an inmate was not required to walk the path was on Sundays, visitors day. I wonder why. Could it have been because the administration were ashamed to leave such a type of punishment open to the public gaze. On Sunday inmates walking the path had to sit under the shed in a group apart.

Length of time on the path varied from a few hours to two and three months.

The time spent in walking the path would approximate three and a half hours a day and at a speed say approaching three miles per hour for each day the inmate spent on the path he would walk at least approximately nine miles (15km). Perhaps ex-warder Dooley was not exaggerating when he says that he saw inmates walking the path with blisters on their feet and blood on their feet. I am inclined to think that he was not.

In my opinion it was an aimless and futile form of punishment and excessively harsh when imposed for long periods. It would not be a deterrent to a potential absconder and would serve no purpose other than to build resentment in the inmate and in its effect of ostracism and silence over all the leisure time, over prolonged periods, it was somewhat akin to solitary confinement.

Hair shorn.

This was a punishment reserved for absconders and attempted absconders and consisted of the whole of the hair of the head being cut off with clippers as close to the scalp as possible. The Superintendent says that this has now been abolished. I would prefer to see it restored. Westbrook is run on the honour system and I see no harm in absconders carrying a shorn head as a badge of shame for a period of one month.

Kangaroo hopping.

This was a punishment mostly imposed by the warders for minor offences such as talking in line, talking in the wards and talking in the recreation room. Again, this punishment when imposed was never entered in the punishment book as required by Reg. 107. It consisted of the inmate, crouched down on his haunches, jumping up and down in a manner similar to a kangaroo's hop. Superintendent Golledge and warder Keates say that the inmate would not be compelled to kangaroo hop for more than a few or five minutes.

Ex-inmate ? claims he has been kangaroo-hopping for one and a half hours and ex-inmate? for three-quarters of an hour with a break in between. I think the periods mentioned by boys have probably been exaggerated but I do think that the punishment has been imposed for longer periods than the five minutes claimed by the Supintendent and warder Keates. The Superintendent informed the Inquiry that kangaroo hopping has now been abolished. According to Inmate ? the last occasion he saw kangaroo hopping was in late March or early April this year when for some reason the Superintendent had the whole ward kangaroo hop in front of their beds. I think the decision to abolish kangaroo hopping is wise. It would impose severe physical strain if imposed for any considerable length of time and it must be rather degrading to compel an inmate, as a punishment, to jump up and down like an animal in front of the other inmates.

Standing out.

This is a punishment imposed by warders for talking on parade or in the wards or in the recreation room and for other minor breaches of discipline such as being slow in undressing. The punishment required the inmate to stand at ease at the foot of his bed or in the recreation room or in the yard for a duration of time to be decided by the particular warder. The rule of silence also applied during the period of his punishment. Again, as in the case of the path punishment, no such punishment was ever recorded in the punishment book as required by Reg. 107. It appears that it is a punishment frequently imposed and as with the path punishment, when imposed, the inmate is not awarded any time certain but remains standing out until released by the warder, which could be at the whim of the warder. Boy ? claims he was stood out at the foot of his bed from 8p.m. until 2a.m. and Boy ? for talking until 2a.m. Ex-inmate ? a truthful witness, saw a boy standing out at midnight and Boy ? was stood out for three hours until 11.30p.m. for changing his blankets for blankets from an unoccupied bed. The worse feature of the Boy ? case is that warder Brose waited until boy ? was warm in bed and on the verge of sleep before ordering him to stand out. Ex-warder Dooley has also seen boys standing out at midnight.

Kneeling to apologise.

Ex-warder Bird makes the startling allegation that he took an inmate named Boy ? to the office for swearing at him. Boy ? is mentally backward. Deputy Superintendent Kolberg was in charge and Bird alleges that the Superintendent gave Boy ? 4 or 5 strikes of the strap and then ordered boy ? to kneel at Mr. Bird's feet and apologise, which boy ? did. This punishment is not recorded in the punishment book. The Deputy Superintendent whilst admitting the unrecorded corporal punishment, denies the kneeling apology.

The punishment book of the 7th January, 1961, contains the following unusual and unexpected record:

Boy ?. Charge backchat.

The record reads 'Boy ? was taken to the office by warder Lowein'. The record continues: 'According to warder this lad gave backchat, but as far as I could ascern there appeared to be a bit of fault on both sides. I made the lad go down on his knees and apologise'.

The entry is under the initials of the Superintendent, Mr. Golledge.

Birthday cake incident.

This refers to an incident that happened at the evening meal. An inmate had his 13th birthday and had received a birthday cake with the customary 13 candles. The cake as required must have been examined and censored and approved by the office, passed to the kitchen, and then on to the inmate's place in the mess room. Ex-warder Greenfield saw the cake with the 13 candles, lit the candles for the boy and told the boy to blow out the candles in the traditional manner. With that, according to the ex-warder, warder cook Hansen 'Raced in, grabbed his hand across the top of the cake, took the icing, candles and all off the top of the cake. What he didn't get the first time he grabbed the second time. He almost wrecked the whole cake'.

Alleged assaults.

Evidence was given in relation to many incidents, too many to deal with in this report. I have selected those incidents which can be called the highlights as I think this cross section will give a picture of conditions existing at Westbrook.

The Superintendent denies that he has ever struck any inmate with his closed fist or ever kicked an inmate.

At transcript the following question was posed to him:

Q. Have you ever struck a boy with closed fists.

A. I admit I have boxed their ears, big cheeky fellows, and 'as I say I have boxed their ears' and again

Q. Did you ever kick a boy.

A. No.

And 'I do not kick boys'.

Unfortunately the Superintendent stands contradicted by his own record in his own hand-writing.

The Schwarten Inquiry—excerpts

The punishment book of 7th February, 1959, contains the following record:

Boy ? Back talk.

Record. 'The matter was referred to me and I spoke to boy ?. After he put his fists up to me when I pushed him away and kicked his behind'.

The punishment book of the 3rd March, 1958, records:

Boy ? Arguing.

Record. Boy ? started arguing with me when I stood him up and I 'floored' him. This soon showed him where he stood and he was civil to'.

As I understand these matters, it would take a blow of considerable force to floor a youth.

Boy ? who was then a member of the dairy party attempted to abscond on the 5th February, 1961. In the morning he climbed into an empty tank through the manhole and hid there during the whole of the day. At 7.30 p.m. that night he climbed out of the tank, was seen by warder Campbell who told him to come down. Instead boy—ran along the roof of the top ward. Schoolteacher Saddler arrived, climbed on the roof after boy ? and boy ? then jumped to the ground, where he was captured by warder Campbell. Boy ? claims that he was then hit several times with a torch across the back of the head by warder Campbell. He says he was then taken around to near the recreation room and claims that there warder Campbell punched him on the side of the head and that he was further punched by schoolteacher Saddler and that he was thrown to the ground and kicked a few times. When he stood up, Superintendent Golledge had arrived and he punched him on the mouth, splitting his lip, and that warder Campbell and schoolteacher Saddler again commenced punching him, and he fell to o the ground where he was kicked in the back by Superintendent Golledge. He was then taken and placed in the recreation room where there was a Baptist Church service in progress. Next morning he received 10 strikes of the strap. Boy ? states that the next morning he reported to the Matron and claims he told her he was beaten up by the Superintendent and two officers.

Apart from such breaches as absconding, discussing absconding, swearing and impudence, corporal punishment has been inflicted for such things as: reading in bed, dropping marbles, making a 'pop' noise with the tongue, eating carrots, not playing football, talking in the bathroom or in wards, making silly remarks, have bread and syrup in bed, taking a piece of bread out of the dining room, supposedly know other inmates intended to abscond, etc.

Saluting.

It is apposite to mention here the practice of saluting, if it can be called saluting. It reminded me of the finger to forelock of the yokel to the village squire; a custom that went out of practice over 100 years ago. The inmates salute is not executed in the orthodox military manner, instead the hand is brought more or less to the front of the hat with the edge of the hand outwards and the hand cut away to the front. I noticed that when an inmate saluted that the warder did not return the salute. Why not ? A salute is a ceremonial act of respect and is always acknowledged by the person paid the compliment by a return of the salute. I also noticed that when saluted, if the warder was in a lounging posture or leaning against a post, that he did not bother to change his posture.

I consider that the practice of the inmate's saluting when he reports back should be abandoned.

The practice of saluting should be reserved for those occasions when a parade is dismissed and the salute should be acknowledged by the warder in charge of the parade.

Boy in haystack incident.

On the 10th May, 1961, inmate ? hid in the haystack with the intention of absconding after dark. He was discovered there by warder Essex. Boy ? states that he was discovered by warder Essex poking into the hay with a pitchfork and that the prong of the pitchfork made a punctured wound in his ankle which later necessitated hospital attention. He further claims that he was pulled from the haystack and thrown from the top to the ground by warder Essex... Boy ? states that he was hidden about two feet down in the haystack...

Schoolteacher Saddler was present when boy ? was discovered. He states that warder Essex was on top of the haystack, that he himself handed Essex the pitchfork which Essex reversed, using only the handle for poking into the hay. Saddler also says that boy ? on discovery was not thrown from the haystack but slid down and there was no suggestion of an injury on boy ?.

Warder Essex says that he was legged up on to the haystack, taking the pitchfork with him. He noticed where the hay appeared to be newly disturbed and that he reversed the pitchfork, using the handle. To scratch the hay away and dig into the hay and discovered boy ?; that he pulled boy ? out and that boy ? then slid to the ground down the side of the Haystack. Warder Essex also pointed out that owing to the top bar of the prongs, the prongs of a pitchfork would not go deeper into the hay than six or seven inches. (18cm)

Inmate ? was at the haystack. He did not see much of the incident, but he heard Mr. Essex call out: 'Here he is' and push him off the haystack.

Pan boys.

A system applies at Westbrook whereby the task of collecting, emptying and cleaning the pans from the earth closets of the officers officers' residences at Westbrook is allotted to the school boys in rotation. One schoolboy's reaction to this chore is, 'I get sick of it, you do it every morning. Sometimes when they get fully loaded it goes all over your hands; when you wash your hands it leaves a smell and you cannot get it off'. I assume that the necessary authority from the Director under Reg.71 has been granted for this work and on that basis I bring this matter forward for consideration as to whether this is a task that should properly be performed by school boys. In my opinion, it is not desirable that school boys should perform this task.

Clothing

The inmates are issued with a change of clothing once a week, on Sunday, and they wear and work in the same clothes continuously from the time of rising in the morning until retiring to bed at night, for the whole week, when they are issued with the previous week's clothes which have been laundered. I am inclined to agree with ex-warder Doorley that, particularly boys in the piggery, dairy and orchard, must be more than smelly. The inmates themselves wash their one pair of socks and one handkerchief in the same open ablution trough in which they all wash their face and clean their teeth, 'though they are instructed to wash the socks and handkerchiefs under the open and running tap. Socks are washed in the afternoon between 4.30p.m. and 5p.m. and are hung at the foot of the bed to dry. If they do not dry overnight the inmates must wear their boots with damp socks or without. Their other clothes are laundered at the laundry. I inspected one lot of laundry that was drying on the line. It is very poorly done. Singlets were a dirty grey, and there was still dirt adhering to singlets, shirts and trousers. As the laundry is done by the inmates mostly young, one is not surprised.

The boots I saw were in good repair condition but unpolished and uncleaned.

Boots are never polished or cleaned and I noticed that the leather in the uppers seemed very hard. They must be uncomfortable and hard on the feet and I believe there is more than a modicum of truth in the statements that they cause blisters, particularly on those inmates who are compelled to walk the inane and senseless punishment of the path. A common complaint of the inmates is that they are not issued with sufficient warm clothing and not early enough. The Commission commenced sitting at Westbrook on the 2nd June, 1961. I was warmly clad with an electric radiator burning in the room but I still felt the cold. I noticed that quite a large number of the inmates were still clad in cotton shorts and singlets and were obviously very cold. A few of the inmates were not wearing jersies or pullovers and some of the pullovers worn were old and thin and had undarned holes. I also made a point of observing the condition of the clothing worn by the inmates. Of 50% of the inmates I regretfully must say that I have never seen a more poverty looking lot. Shirts, shorts and trousers had been considerably patched and patches had been repatched. Seams were pulling apart and a lot were threadbare. Quite a lot were ill-fitting. In this dress there is no build-up of morale or self-respect.

Food.

Regulation 6 requires that a copy of the dietary scale approved shall be hung in the dining room. This has not been carried out.

Reg.56 reads: 'The cook shall be held responsible for the cooking and preparation of all meals and for the cleanliness and good condition of the kitchen and all its appliances'.

This Regulation also has not been fully carried out, as the following meals are solely prepared by the 8–10 inmates comprising the kitchen party for the period; every breakfast, the evening meal on every Wednesday, and all main meals on every Saturday and Sunday. At these times the warder cook is off duty in conformity of working a 40 hour week. Since the commencement of the inquiry there has been a change, in that the warder cook now comes on duty sufficiently early to be in the kitchen for the preparation of breakfast. Complaints by the inmates were that the diet was monotonous, food was badly cooked, hot meals were cold when they reached the inmates, the porridge on occasions was weevily, there were grubs in the vegetables and dried fruits, and maggots in the meat used in the stews.

The complaints that at times the food was badly cooked, are justified. I do not see how it could be otherwise. The warder cook is not properly trained and when he goes on recreation leave he is relieved by another warder also without training as a cook. Also, under the present system the responsibility for the preparation and cooking of meals does to a large extent fall upon the young untrained inmates who themselves are changed every three months when a new kitchen party marches in.

The allegation regarding the dried fruit infestation was rather startlingly proved correct by inmate witness Boy ?. I had the sultanas and currants and the grubs identified and analysed and the State Analyst certified that the washed product (sultanas and currants) were unfit for human consumption.

Accommodation.

I inspected the wards and certainly they were overcrowded, beds being much too close together with the number of inmates (130) it had to be. The wards were clean but did appear drab and cheerless and would be cold. The quilts appeared to be dirty and I thought had not been laundered for quite a long time. The sheets also had that dirty grey look about them. Each bed had five blankets but I noticed that a large number of the blankets appeared to be very new and a large proportion of the old blankets appeared to be rather threadbare.

Showers.

It is quite obvious that the cutting off of the hot water is a punishment to one or more inmates breaking the rules of silence. Being compelled to take a cold shower in a Toowoomba winter, to put it mildly, would not be pleasant. There are two things wrong with this practice, firstly it is an unauthorised form of punishment, and secondly a punishment imposed in such a way that the innocent are made to suffer with the guilty.

Nowhere do the Regulations say that an inmate can be compelled to shower in cold water for some breach of discipline and nowhere do the Regulations authorise the punishing of the innocent because the guilty cannot be pinpointed and ascertained. Methods such as this must build resentment and they should be abandoned.

I am somewhat intrigued as to why the rule of silence is imposed at the bath house during this period.

General.

After hearing all the witnesses and perusing the punishment book I was left with the opinion that the atmosphere at Westbrook was retributive and repressive, where even laughter was frowned upon.

I was left with the opinion. that the strap was used excessively and over-severely as witnessed by the red weals seen by ex-warder Dooley on the seven boys involved in the grape incident and as witnessed by the weals and contused and risen veins on boy ?'s arm , and the scarring of boys (about 20 mentioned).

I also have the opinion that there is some truth in the inmates' other allegations of striking and kicking and not referred to by me elsewhere in this report but referred to in the transcript at p.14 kicking of schoolboy and dark boy, p.337,338, 417 hitting of inmate, p.488 banging of inmate ?'s head against wall, p.479 hitting of inmate ? p.532 striking of inmate ? across the ear with a strap, p.802 hitting of inmate ? p.947,1039,1241 striking of inmate ? p.1109,1119,1103 striking of inmate ? with hoe handle, p.1261 slapping of inmate ? on his head, and p.1220 slapping of inmate ?.

Apart from the sworn testimony of the witnesses I am fortified in this belief by the unrestrained and intemperate expressions used quite frequently in the punishment book.

Correlating Appendix 5 with Appendix 6 shows that there were 248 strappings of 98 individual inmates for the year ended 31st December 1959, 329 strappings of 133 individual inmates for the year ended 31st December 1960 and for the four and a half months from 1 January 1961. to the 13 May 1961, 199 strappings of 93 individual inmates.

What percentage of the population of Westbrook was strapped over the respective periods shown in the appendices cannot be determined as the number of inmates is not static, some being admitted, some being discharged, but on the basis that the static population would be somewhere about 100, it would appear that very few inmates escaped corporal punishment.

Recidivism.

I have attached herewith Appendix 4 which is a statement of the post-criminal history of ex-inmates of Westbrook. The appendix is compiled from Ex.22 and covers inmates discharged from the Institution for the approximately 4 years period from 1st July 1957 to the 14th May 1961.

Over that approximately four years period, 290 inmates were discharged. Of that 290, 131 or 45% were, in Queensland, subsequently convicted of one or more criminal offences.

As Appendix 4 shows, these 131 recidivists between them committed a large total of 719 criminal offences, the offences, amongst others, ranging from one of wilful murder to 287 of stealing, 129 of breaking, entering and stealing, and 129 of unlawfully using a motor vehicle.

The total of 719 offences averages 5.5 offences per each convicted ex-inmate, but of course some were convicted only once and others five or six times, but considering their young age group the total of 719 offences is very large.

I do not think that any parallel can be drawn between the Westbrook figure of 45% and the Borstal figures, as the Borstal statistics cover age groups from 16 years to 21 years on sentence, whereas the Westbrook figures covers only the 14 years to 18 years age group and on discharge, most Westbrook inmates would not have attained their 18th birthday.

I would anticipate that lapse into crime would be greater amongst the older age group than amongst the younger age group. The Borstal figures show a steady decline and I think that if it was possible to obtain a comparison by age groups, say of the16 years to 18 years group, of dischargees from Westbrook and Borstal, with the total number of offences committed, that it would be found that the Westbrook figures of recidivism would be much worse than the comparable figures of Borstal.

In my opinion the recovery rate of Westbrook must be considered as unsatis-factory.

AE Schwarten